Tarot Disassembled Guidebook

DECONSTRUCTING THE SYMBOLS OF THE MAJOR AND MINOR ARCANA

Jennifer Cooper Steidley

foreword by Theresa Reed

This edition first published in 2024 by Weiser Books, an imprint of
Red Wheel/Weiser, LLC
With offices at:
65 Parker Street, Suite 7
Newburyport, MA 01950
www.redwheelweiser.com

A previous edition was published in 2023 by Jennifer Cooper Steidley/Ferocious Ink

ISBN 978-1-57863-864-2

Library of Congress Cataloging-in-Publication Data available upon request.

Typeset in Cormorant Garamond

Printed in the United States of America
IBI

10 9 8 7 6 5 4 3 2 1

Contents

Major Arcana

Minor Arcana

SUIT OF WANDS

SUIT OF CUPS

SUIT OF SWORDS

SUIT OF PENTACLES

For my son, Emmett,
who inspired this deck and inspires me
to see the world in new ways every day.

Foreword

Tarot is the language of symbols. Much like a child's picture book, you can begin to understand the cards' meanings by simply looking at the images.

Most folks can recall the first time they started to read books. I was an early reader, thanks to an unexpected six-week stay in the hospital when I was two years old. I had broken my leg, which meant being stuck in traction. Of course, I was bored out of my little skull, with nothing to do except watch *Sesame Street* and page through the books the nurses gave me.

By the time I was out of the hospital, I was walking . . . and reading.

When I discovered tarot, I was a typical teen with a rebellious streak and lack of purpose. I nabbed my first deck on impulse, drawn in by the art and the burning desire to know my future. At the time, the only tarot deck in the store was the Marseilles. The woodcut images intrigued me, but the task of deciphering what they meant felt like an onerous chore, mainly because I didn't connect to the art. (I also didn't have a teacher or a "tarot *Sesame Street*" to guide me.)

My journey took a significant turn when I acquired a Rider-Waite-Smith deck a few months later. This deck's art, which resonated with me, was just the beginning. As I delved deeper into the cards, I noticed intricate details that demanded my attention. These details sparked interpretations, fueling what would become a lifelong passion.

The little white dog hinted at caution, the flower in the Fool's hand suggested purity, while the bag indicated the past—or perhaps a bag of tricks? These symbols, I discovered, were not random occurrences but intentional elements woven into the fabric of the deck.

This realization sparked a curiosity in me. Was this an accident? How did this tie the cards together . . . or not?

The desire to find the correlations has had me on many tarot wild-goose chases ever since. In fact, I've even recently found symbols I didn't know existed after blowing up the cards for a coloring book. Even so, that only gave me part of the picture.

Enter *Tarot Disassembled*, a unique deck that caught my eye when I first saw it being used on social media. This deck, unlike traditional ones, is stripped down to the core elements of each card. It presents *only* the symbols, with no pictures of human figures in motion. At first, this seems almost blasphemous! How might this minimalist approach impact my understanding of tarot? More importantly, how would this deck read? I needed to know.

Once I had a copy in my hands, I realized the brilliance of Jennifer Cooper Steidley's concept. All you have to go on are the traditional symbols for the card. Nothing is obvious, yet it is. After all, these are archetypal symbols we all recognize, much like simple images in picture books. When you dive in, you start to see the cards like you have never seen them before.

By breaking each card down to the basics, you are free to explore new interpretations of universal symbols. For instance, the rich green background in the Queen of Pentacles symbolizes growth and prosperity. The rabbit represents fertility, the crown signifies leadership, and the fruits indicate a harvest. From those clues, you can see the meanings unfold, much like the letters in words.

But like language, the symbols in the *Tarot Disassembled* deck come together in surprising ways. For example, the Queen of Pentacles has a goat head in the upper right-hand corner, which can also be seen in The Emperor and The Devil. This shared symbol suggests an interesting connection between the three cards, hinting at a story of power, wealth, and greed. Is the Queen here to lead, or is she concerned with her own selfish interests? Is she a gold digger? These connections between cards add depth and complexity to the reading, inviting further exploration and interpretation.

Once you start seeing these subtle links between cards in *Tarot Disassembled*, you cannot unsee them. Instead, you become even more tarot-fluent. It's like taking the deck apart and putting it back together in a whole new way, inventing a new language from an old one. This process of disassembling the cards and finding new connections has enriched my understanding of tarot and sparked my intuition in new ways. *Tarot Disassembled* is a modern and clever update on a classic and sure to inspire your own tarot journey.

—Theresa Reed,
author of *The Cards You're Dealt*

Introduction

Welcome to *Tarot Disassembled!* In early 2021, I had a lightbulb moment while watching my son disassemble his sandwich into its various ingredients so that he could analyze them more closely. As I watched him, I pondered the potential for deeper understanding that lies in the act of disassembling. Since my brain is forever obsessed with all things tarot related, I began considering how deconstructing the tarot could enhance our understanding of it. In that moment, the idea for *Tarot Disassembled* was born.

This book is a guide to the cards of *Tarot Disassembled*, but it also stands alone as a sourcebook for the symbolism in the tarot. The new Weiser Books editions of both the deck and guidebook contain some significant updates from my earlier self-published edition: the two have been updated to reflect new things that I have learned since the creation of the first edition. (Tarot is such an amazingly multilayered system, that I imagine the learning never truly ends. That's half the fun!) There are 13 new symbols that have been added, as well as numerous changes to small details with big meaning; for example, updating the number of rays on the sun in both the Fool card and the Sun card, as well as introducing purple to the color palette. Every alteration I have made has meaning, and I have tried to reflect that in each card's information.

I strongly encourage you to obtain the *Tarot Disassembed* deck. Even though this guidebook will be illuminating for tarot symbolism generally, you will get much more out of the experience using it with the deck of the same name. This book has been produced in black and white, and I make many references to color in the cards. These are colors that show up in the Rider-Waite-Smith system of tarot, but you'll find this book most rewarding when used as a one-to-one match with the *Tarot Disassembled* tarot.

A LITTLE BIT ABOUT ME

I have worked professionally as a graphic designer for 30 years and have been fascinated by tarot for longer. I am also an avid deck collector and self-proclaimed research nerd; I adore the process of taking a deep dive into any subject that holds my interest. Dissecting the layers within a single symbol satisfies something within me.

The common thread between graphic design and tarot is the language of symbolism. For as long as I can remember, symbology has held a special fascination for me. It's a visual language that I understand somewhere in my core. It's what drew me to my career as a graphic designer and what started my love affair with tarot from the first moment I laid eyes on a deck.

A (VERY) BRIEF HISTORY OF THE TAROT

This deck is based on the symbology of the Rider-Waite-Smith tarot. For those of you new to tarot, the Rider-Waite-Smith (RWS) deck is a relatively modern deck in the history of tarot as a whole. But it is arguably the most iconic and widely circulated deck in the world and the basis for the majority of modern decks created since the RWS first came on the scene in 1910.

I won't go too deep into the history of tarot here. There are a multitude of books and resources out there to learn tarot history from, and I absolutely encourage you to seek them out. But I will say that tarot has a long, complex, and somewhat mysterious history. The tarot as we know it can be traced back to the 1400s in Italy (most notably the Visconti-Sforza Tarot), but its legacy extends even further back with its genesis in the game of *tarocchi* in the 1300s.

The 78 cards that comprise the tarot are structured into two arcana: there are 22 Major Arcana cards and 56 Minor Arcana cards. Further, these 56 Minor Arcana are divided into four suits of 14 cards each. The Minor Arcana follows a structure similar to a pack of standard playing cards: each suit comprising cards ace through 10, and four court cards. The Minor Arcana deals with everyday, mundane situations in life while the Major Arcana deals with the bigger-picture, esoteric concepts. The 22 cards of the Major Arcana portray universal archetypes from the Fool through the World. The Major Arcana is also seen as a story of the Hero's Journey as the Fool travels from card 0 to card 21.

In 1910, the Rider-Waite-Smith tarot deck was published for the first time by Rider and Co. Envisioned by Arthur E. Waite and beautifully illustrated and brought to life by Pamela Colman Smith, this deck was unique in that it was the first time the pip cards of the Minor Arcana included pictorial scenes rather than just the numbers of each card in the suit. Waite and Smith were both members of the Hermetic Order of the Golden Dawn, a secret society dedicated to the study of the occult and metaphysics. The rich imagery woven into the RWS tarot was influenced by Qabalah, Freemasonry, alchemy, Christian and Jewish mysticism, and spiritual antiquity.

HOW TO USE THIS BOOK AND DECK

My primary goal in creating the deck and writing this companion guidebook was to deconstruct the traditional symbolism found in the RWS deck and strive to uncover deeper meaning within the individual symbols. I have tried to do a deep dive into some of the connotations, but symbols are like onions—there are layers and layers to be uncovered within each one.

This book presents the most commonly known associations with each symbol as well as my own ideas and correspondences . . . some of which may not be immediately obvious but I feel provide additional layers of meaning. To a large degree, there are no right or wrong answers in tarot, but I invite you to enjoy going down the rabbit hole with me! If this book draws out one single, "ooh, how interesting!" from you, then I've accomplished my mission. You'll find my writing style to be at times direct and to the point, at other times whimsical and playful, and at still other times downright irreverent. Take it all with a grain of salt, but most importantly, enjoy the journey.

INDIVIDUAL CARD PAGES

There is a section dedicated to each of the 78 cards in the deck. For each card I have provided the following:

* **Keywords.** These terms summarize the energy of the card. Keywords are neutral; they embody both the upright and reversed energy of the card. In the *Reversed* entries, I extrapolate on a keyword's potential shadow quality or "flipped" meaning if applicable.

* **Astrological Associations, Planetary Associations, and Elemental Associations.** Some cards do not have both an astrological and planetary association, and some have multiple. I've made notations when this is the case. Also, most of the cards in the deck have a single corresponding element based on their suit (Wands = fire, Cups = water, Swords = air, Pentacles = earth), except for the Court cards, which embody both the element of their suit as well as the element specific to them (Pages = earth, Knights = fire, Queens = water, Kings = air).

* **Individual Symbols.** I have deconstructed each card into its individual symbols. I then provide analysis of the meaning of the symbols. In some cases, I include keywords only for the symbol and in other cases I go on for several paragraphs. While I was writing this book, the symbols really took on a life of their own. Some had a big story to tell, while others were quieter and simpler. Please note that you might find some symbols not addressed at all on a particular card. The Death card (13) is one such example: you'll notice that I have chosen to include imagery of the tower on the card, but provide no analysis of this symbol in the discussion of the card. But wait—soon you'll come to The Tower card (17) and you'll have the aha moment as you discover one type of transformation leading to another. This is what I'm referring to when I speak of symbols being like onions—tarot, especially, needs to be explored layer by layer, discovering meanings upon meanings. When you find a symbol that

you're particularly struck by, please refer to the index of symbols at the back of this book to see where else it occurs.

- **Quick Takes.** Each card section ends with an entry of "quick takes." Written in fragmented form, this entry is intended to give possible scenarios, actions, and situations that the card might imply in a reading. These can be particularly useful if you are new to tarot or are in a rush and don't have time to delve into the depth of the individual symbols.

A NOTE ABOUT REVERSALS

A *reversal* refers to a card appearing upside down in a reading. In the tarot community, there are a variety of stances on whether and how to read card reversals. Some readers do not work with them at all; others do. Personally, I see reversals as another way opposing dualities present themselves in our world. Day can't exist without night; light can't exist without dark; etc. I believe all of these cards have a shadow side to their energy—just as we do. When I read for myself, I will take into consideration the reversed meaning when a card shows up this way. But I will also discount it when it doesn't feel relevant. (I will also take into consideration the reversed meaning of a card even when it's right side up if it feels pertinent to the energy of the situation.) Again, there are no right or wrong ways to work with tarot, so I say do what feels authentic to you and your current experience.

FINAL THOUGHTS

Whether you are just starting your tarot adventure or are an avid tarot connoisseur, thank you for making *Tarot Disassembled* part of your journey! If I've learned anything about tarot, it's that you could devote all of your years on this Earth to the study of tarot and still only scratch the surface. I highly recommend you seek out as many avenues of learning on the subject as possible—you'll find an abundance of resources available. I hope you will find this deck, and tarot in general, to be an amazing tool for your spiritual growth.

Exercises & Spreads

First and foremost, let me preface this discussion on spreads by saying there is no right or wrong way to work with a tarot deck. It's all about using your intuition, so above all, let that be your guide. There are a plethora of ideas, resources, and spreads available for working with any deck, and I highly recommend you explore what's out there. What I've included here are just a few recommendations to get you started with the *Tarot Disassembled* deck—feel free to customize these to fit your mood. In general, I recommend approaching this deck with the energy of the Fool . . . be playful, curious, open to what comes up, and dive right in!

Let's start with some exercises.

STUDY BUDDY

This is a simple one. Whip out a Rider-Waite-Smith deck (or a deck in the RWS style), pull a card, and lay it side by side with a *Tarot Disassembled* card. Examine them closely. Notice what symbols in the RWS card come to your attention that you may have never noticed before. Journal or make notes about your impressions.

SYMBOL SYNCHRONICITIES

This exercise is best done first thing in the morning but can be tried at any time of day. Shuffle the *Tarot Disassembled* deck any way you see fit. Fan the cards out or cut the deck and draw a single card. Look at the card. What symbol do you notice first? It may be larger, or it may be one of the tiny ones on the card. Whatever your eye goes to first, that is the symbol to focus on for the day. Go about your regular routine and pay particular attention to where you notice this symbol popping up in other areas of your life. For example, you may have chosen grapes as your symbol. Maybe you see them at the grocery store, or maybe they appear on a billboard as you drive around town. Perhaps a coworker is wearing a necklace with a grape pendant that day. You may be surprised what synchronicities occur when your intuition homes in on that symbol. At the end of the day, write down all of the things that came up for you when you saw that symbol. When you're done, dig into the book to see what it has to say about it (at the end of this book you'll find an index of symbols so you can easily find which cards they appear in). How did your impressions compare to the information in the book?

Alternatively, you can choose to work with the book and card in tandem as soon as you draw that card. But the first method makes this more of an intuitive exercise, and you may just be surprised at what intuitive hits you get.

FOLLOW THE LEADER

Shuffle your deck any way you see fit. Cut the cards once, restack them, and draw the top card. Choose a symbol on the card. Now, starting with the top card on your face down deck, start flipping cards over until you find your chosen symbol again. Keep going until you find another. Now lay the three cards out side by side and continue with a typical three-card reading of your choice. The example on the following page shows mountains.

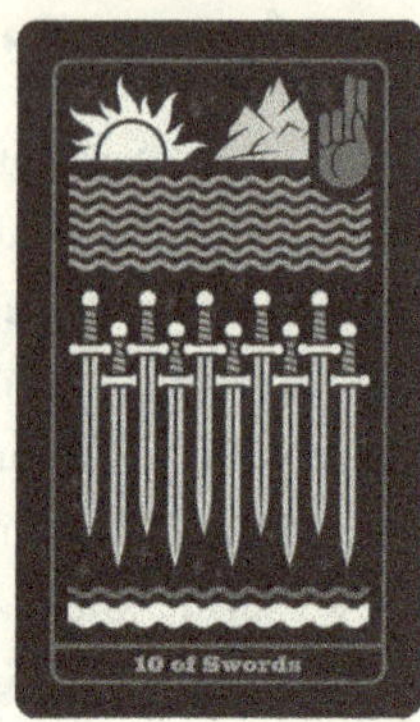

Now let's turn our attention to a couple suggested layouts to get you started on your disassembled journey.

The Destruction/Creation Spread is a simple two-card draw. When you read it, pay special attention to how the symbolism may change or be different from card to card. For example, the mountains of the Strength card are small in size compared to other cards, and perhaps less daunting to tackle. On the other hand, the snowy, icy mountains found in the Hermit card indicate they are in a place of isolation and solitude. How does knowing this deeper symbolism affect your understanding of the reading?

Approach the Fully Assembled Spread in the same way, allowing yourself to sink deeply into the added flavor and information that the cards' symbolism brings.

Destruction/Creation Spread

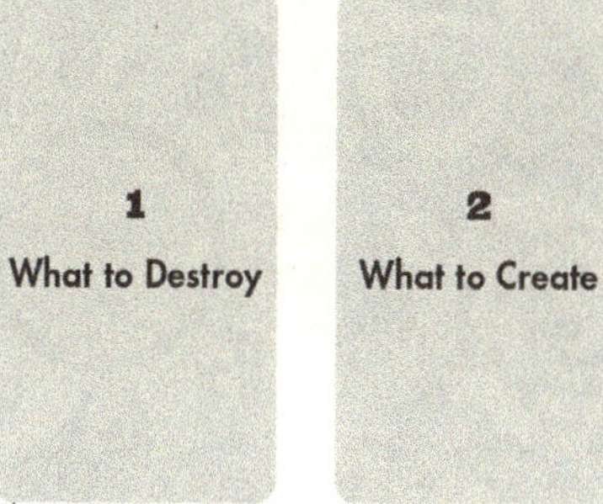

The Fully Assembled Spread

4
What will it look like reassembled?

2
What part needs to be discarded?

1
What needs to be disassembled at this time?

3
What part needs to be added?

Major Arcana

0. The Fool

KEYWORDS: new beginnings, potential, innocence, joy, freedom, optimism, spontaneity, adventure, inexperience, risk, foolishness

ASSOCIATIONS

Astrological: none

Planetary: Uranus

Elemental: air

Symbols

NUMBER ZERO: pure potential. This applies beautifully to the Fool who is poised at the beginning of a great journey where anything could happen. (It is worth noting that numerically, there is still some disagreement about whether the Fool belongs at the beginning or the end of the Major Arcana. The shape of the number zero itself hints at the true nature of the Major Arcana as a never-ending cycle as opposed to a linear journey with a definitive end.)

BACKPACK/SATCHEL: survival, baggage, hidden talents. The satchel the Fool carries can represent what we choose to carry with us on our journey (literal emotional "baggage") or even undiscovered talents and abilities we have yet to explore. Either way, rest assured we are all equipped with the bare essentials needed for our journey.

BOOT: action, journey, travel, grounding, connection to the earth, humanity, consciousness. Yellow is the color of the solar plexus chakra, the seat of our personal power and self-confidence. These vibrant yellow boots indicate that even though the Fool may appear to be acting impulsively, they may simply be so sure of themselves that they do not fear where their next steps may take them . . . a true leap of faith!

CLIFF: danger, risks, challenges, jumping-off point, threshold, faith, unknown, decisions. The cliff is a potent symbol that perfectly sums up the dual nature of the Fool. Is the Fool simply an idiot that doesn't realize the danger they are in on the edge of that precipice? Or do they know something we do not? Are they so enlightened that they are without fear? Keep in mind the Fool's number is zero, which means they may be at the beginning of the journey or at the end, having traveled through the entire Major Arcana. So it's entirely possible the cliff holds no fear for them anymore—they've attained enough wisdom to understand that anything worth doing comes with a touch of risk. I think this quote by Ray Bradbury says it best: "First you jump off the cliff and you build your wings on the way down."

DOG: loyalty, protection, domestication, unconditional love. Interpretations of the white dog found on The Fool card vary from faithful companion to protector, potentially warning of what practical disaster might await off the edge of that cliff. Personally, when I picture a typical domesticated dog, I think of their sweet ability to love wholeheartedly and unconditionally, regardless of their primitive animal nature. So I see the white dog as the purest representation of hope and faith. Dogs are also strong symbols of protection due to the way they will loyally defend their pack (human or fur-based) at all costs. This indicates that the Fool is not in any true danger, but rather divinely protected on his journey.

EAGLE: vision, divine messenger, expanded consciousness, flight, leadership, majesty, authority, transcendence, astrological sign of Scorpio. In the original RWS tarot, it's easy to miss the tiny eagle that adorns the Fool's satchel. But as small as this symbol is, it packs a powerful punch. Much as the lion is the "king of the beasts," the eagle is inarguably the king of the sky. Eagles are highly revered in many cultures for their power, supreme vision, and, with the soaring heights they fly at, their closeness to the heavenly realm. They are also considered to be one of the forms of the astrological sign of Scorpio. Unlike any other sign in the zodiac, Scorpio takes more than one form. The eagle is the higher expression of Scorpio . . . transcending from the crawling, earthbound scorpion to the soaring bird of prey. This makes me think the Fool, who is traditionally perched on a high cliff, is totally in their comfort zone. The eagle symbolizes the expanded consciousness and transcendence that the Fool attains on their cyclical journey through the Major Arcana and back again. (The "Fool" moniker is starting to seem more and more like a clever ruse . . . they might just be the wisest and most divine figure in the deck.)

FEATHER: element of air, freedom, hope, travel, ease of movement, lightheartedness, spiritual evolution, truth. The Fool embodies the feather's qualities of lightheartedness and freedom. The sense of movement symbolized by the feather also comes into play here, as the Fool is embarking on a great journey. (Though it may be more of a spiritual journey than a literal one.) The vibrant red color of the Fool's feather is emblematic of both their fiery life force and their willingness to passionately charge ahead.

Interestingly, scientists have proven that if you drop a bowling ball and a feather at the same time inside a vacuum, they will hit the ground at the same time. Normally, it's the air resistance that affects how quickly each object falls. In tarot, air is the element of the mental realm. It is also the element associated with this card. Perhaps the gentle feather serves as a reminder that to be lighthearted also requires keeping our thoughts light.

MOUNTAINS: challenges, obstacles. As the Fool is at the beginning of a new journey, the mountains simply reflect the fact that no journey worth taking is ever a straight line.

ROSE: passion, vitality, enlightenment, secret wisdom, unfolding, magic, illumination, transformation. The white rose found on the Fool card is sometimes referred to as the "rose of transformation," alluding to the spiritual growth that awaits from embarking on this unknown adventure. White is also the color of purity, indicating the pure intentions and innocence of the Fool.

In Eastern traditions, the rose is linked to the heart chakra—the energetic center of love for ourselves and others—as well as empathy, compassion, and forgiveness. The love energy of the heart chakra is deeper than mere romantic love. It encompasses the unconditional love we feel for those we are most connected to as well as the love we give to ourselves. The unfolding rose can symbolize the Fool's openhearted nature. In order to experience love more fully, we must similarly strive to open our own hearts—a process that almost always begins with self-love.

STAFF: support, guidance, leadership, pilgrimage, solitude, conduit, union of opposites, magic, healing. The staff of the Fool is black in color, representing the unknowns of the journey they are embarking upon. In my opinion, the presence of the staff symbol brings a spiritual depth to the Fool that might otherwise appear to be missing. The staff resonates with magical energy, acting as a conduit between the earthly realm and the spiritual realms. Some texts say that simply holding a staff would allow the bearer access to information from higher realms. With its tie to pilgrims and saints, it also represents a sense of leadership, suggesting that there might just be a dose of wisdom embedded in the foolishness of the Fool.

SUN: life force, joy, optimism, vitality, growth, cycles, illumination, alchemy. The sun of the Fool card is unique in that it white in color. An interesting scientific tidbit—though we perceive the sun as yellow, the actual color of the sun is white. The white sun shown on the Fool card hints at the enlightenment that the Fool either has the potential to attain or already has. Reinforcing this further, the white sun is also said to be associated with Kether, the "crown" that is the topmost sephirah on the Qabalistic Tree of Life diagram. Count carefully and you will also notice that there are exactly 14 rays on the sun, which just happens to be the number of the Temperance card. Temperance is the card of alchemy. This intentional nod to the alchemy of the Temperance card suggests that the Fool has initiated a journey of high-level transformation.

WHEEL: spiritual progression, forward movement, law, cycle of rebirth. The eight-spoked wheel is traditionally found repeated as a pattern on the Fool's tunic. Sometimes referred to as the "spirit wheel," this symbol is found in several ancient world cultures. In Buddhism, it is a symbol of spiritual progression or "the noble eightfold path." Interestingly, it is also sometimes described as being the wheel of a chariot. (What an awesome infusion of Chariot card energy!) This reinforces the Fool's path toward enlightenment and suggests they are leveling up at a rapid rate!

QUICK TAKES: Just do it! Dream big, create new beginnings, seize unlimited potential, take a leap of faith, make that big life change you've been wanting to make. It's time to release old baggage, approach the situation with openness and curiosity, travel the world, have a "yes" day, listen to your inner child, do something that scares you. Come out; try skydiving or cliff jumping, adopt a dog.

REVERSED: *worry and anxiety holding you back, playing it too safe, overanalyzing a situation, know the difference between being reckless and being bold, adulting too hard.*

1. The Magician

KEYWORDS: manifestation, success, resourcefulness, will, trickery, manipulation, indecision

ASSOCIATIONS

Astrological: none

Planetary: Mercury

Elemental: air

Symbols

NUMBER ONE: beginnings, initiation, confidence. The shape of the number one is reflected in the double-tipped wand of the Magician.

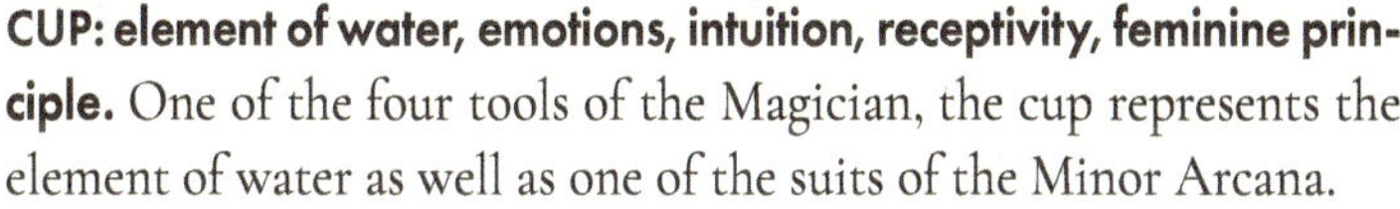

CUP: element of water, emotions, intuition, receptivity, feminine principle. One of the four tools of the Magician, the cup represents the element of water as well as one of the suits of the Minor Arcana.

DOUBLE-TIPPED WAND: divine inspiration, spiritual wisdom, will, conduit, harmony, perfect union, balance. If we think of a traditional magician's wand, it channels and focuses the user's energy. The powerful double-tipped wand of the Magician focuses not only their intention and will but also connects the spiritual realm with the material plane. ("As above, so below.") The meaning of equilibrium also comes heavily into play here . . . one cannot create magic without carefully balancing all the forces and elements involved.

Those who work with crystals might see a resemblance between the double-tipped wand and the naturally occurring double-terminated crystal. Crystals like quartz can sometimes form with a point on each end. This shape allows energy to flow both ways, absorbing it on one end, transmuting it, and then emanating it out the other end. The double-tipped wand can work the same way.

GREENERY: abundance, growth.

LEMNISCATE (INFINITY SYMBOL): infinity, eternity, perpetual motion, limitlessness, balance. In the simplest terms, this mathematical symbol represents that which is boundless or endless. For the Magician, this means their potential to create and manifest has no limits.

LILY: purity, knowledge, feminine principle, fertility, rebirth. For the Magician, the white lily represents the purity of their intention. The combination of lilies and roses together on one card symbolizes the balancing of feminine and masculine energies that is required to create magic.

OUROBOROS (SNAKE EATING ITS TAIL): eternity, rebirth, cycles, unity. The ouroboros is a widely used ancient symbol with roots in ancient Egypt. (The oldest known appearance of this symbol was in King Tutankhamun's tomb.) The Egyptians had a keen understanding of time as a repeating series of cycles rather than simply linear, evidenced by the yearly flooding of the Nile and the journey of the sun. The Gnostics interpreted the opposing ends of the ouroboros to represent the material and the spiritual . . . seemingly opposing forces that are interconnected, symbolizing humanity's eternal unity with the divine.

PENTACLE: element of earth, physical or material realm, money and material possessions, five elements, harmony, protection, nature, feminine principle. One of the four tools of the Magician, the pentacle represents the element of earth as well as one of the suits of the Minor Arcana.

ROSE: passion, vitality, enlightenment, secret wisdom, unfolding, magic, illumination, transformation, masculine principle. The rose has long been revered by all kinds of ancient orders and cultures as a secret symbol of unfolding wisdom. A rose in full bloom can be seen to represent the attainment of spiritual enlightenment. The rose holds a special place as a symbol for the Rosicrucian Order, a secret society that Arthur E. Waite, cocreator of the RWS tarot, just so happened to belong to. Coincidence? I think not. The medieval term *sub rosa* (Latin for "under the rose") was used to describe secret, confidential information. These elements of secrecy linked to the rose represent the secret wisdom the Magician has access to, enabling their magic.

SWORD: element of air, intellect, power, discernment, decisiveness, truth, purification, masculine principle. One of the four tools of the Magician, the sword represents the element of air as well as one of the suits of the Minor Arcana.

Possibly the most legendary sword of myth is the great Excalibur. This magical sword is said to have been pulled out of a rock by Arthur—the boy who was to become king—when no one else could. In the Volsunga Saga of Icelandic lore, we find another special sword: At a wedding, the Norse god Odin thrusts a sword named Gramr into a tree and announces that anyone able to remove the blade will find no better weapon anywhere. All the guests take turns trying to dislodge it, but only a warrior named Sigmund succeeds. As swords are associated with our thoughts, I can't help but think that what Arthur and Sigmund have in common is that they both thought themselves worthy. The sword of the Magician card is a sharp reminder that to accomplish true magic, we must train our thoughts to believe in our own badassery.

TABLE: material world, grounding. Manifestation cannot take place in the spiritual realm alone. The table represents the need to ground our thoughts and desires in the earthly plane to make something a reality.

WAND: element of fire, spiritual realm, masculine principle. One of the four tools of the Magician, the branch-like wand represents the element of fire as well as one of the suits of the Minor Arcana.

QUICK TAKES: Your manifestation game is on point right now, and you have all the tools you need to succeed. Believe in yourself and watch the magic unfold. You're capable of anything. Speak your intentions out loud and think about what you want to create in your life; your words and thoughts have power—summon your will-power.

REVERSED: *manifesting negativity, someone is conning you, beware of false illusions, careful what you wish for, lacking resources.*

2. The High Priestess

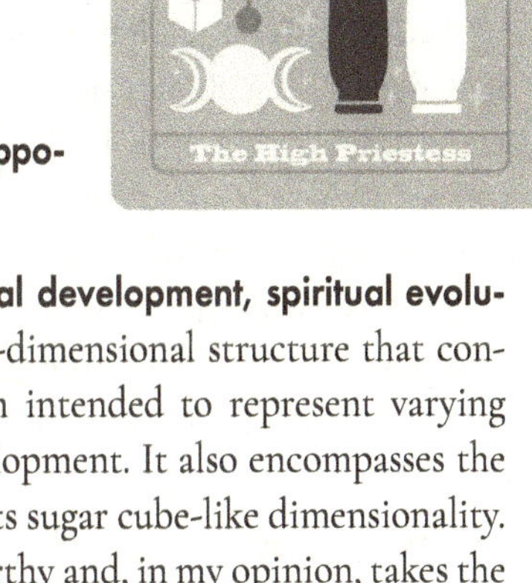

KEYWORDS: intuition, mystery, subconscious, divine feminine, duality, wisdom, secrets, disconnection

ASSOCIATIONS

Astrological: none

Planetary: moon

Elemental: water

Symbols

NUMBER TWO: duality, balance, opposition, harmony.

CUBE: initiation, dominion, spiritual development, spiritual evolution. The Cube of Space is a three-dimensional structure that contains a dizzyingly complex system intended to represent varying degrees or grades of spiritual development. It also encompasses the 22 Major Arcana cards of tarot in its sugar cube-like dimensionality. This one is definitely deep dive-worthy and, in my opinion, takes the High Priestess's sacred wisdom game to the next level.

EQUAL-ARMED CROSS: balance, peace, oneness. Sometimes referred to as the Greek cross, the equal-armed cross has held different meanings in a variety of cultures in history. For the ancient Celts, it represented the meeting place of divine energies; in ancient Greece, the four elements. To the Ancestral Pueblo of North America and in the ancient Middle East, it represented the four directions (north, east, south, and west.)

MOON: intuition, cycles, emotions, divine feminine, subconscious, shadow work, reflection, hidden information.

PALM TREE: abundance, fruitfulness, hope, wisdom. The date palm is associated with Hathor, Egyptian goddess of love and fertility and another representation of the divine feminine. It is also a tree that can thrive in dry, harsh conditions symbolizing the ability to survive the challenges life throws your way. The fruit—dates—also mimic the shape of the pineal gland, which is thought to be the key to higher states of consciousness.

The palm tree is also linked to wisdom, which the High Priestess has in abundance. As early as 500 BCE, people from the Middle East to the Far East used palm leaves instead of paper to write down their stories and thoughts. Consider the palm tree a leafy nudge to record and share your own wisdom.

POMEGRANATE: abundance, fertility, womb, divine feminine, wisdom, death. Persephone was forced to forever spend half of the year in the Underworld with Hades after having dined on pomegranate seeds. There is also a belief that the pomegranate was the original "forbidden fruit" of the Tree of Knowledge that Adam and Eve ingested. What do these two stories have in common? In both, the pomegranate can be seen to have initiated the eater into a higher level of knowledge. Persephone became privy to the well-guarded secrets of the Underworld, while Adam and Eve were initiated into the wisdom of the Tree of Knowledge. While the pomegranate here symbolizes all of the lushness of the divine feminine, it can also be seen to signify the secret knowledge and mysteries that the High Priestess watches over.

SCROLL: guidance, wisdom, knowledge. In a general sense, scrolls typically represent important information or knowledge yet to be learned. Since the scroll is partially rolled up, it adds to the High Priestess's energy of mystery and hidden secrets. In the traditional RWS tarot, it is shown with *TORA* written on it, believed by many to be representative of the Hebrew word for "direction and instruction." But a deeper dive into the possible layers of meaning held by these four letters reveals their anagrams: *rota* is Latin for "wheel" (cycles), *taro* is a shortened form of "tarot," *orat* has Latin roots meaning "to speak" (or teach), and *ator* can be seen as a simplified pronunciation of Hathor, Egyptian goddess of love and fertility. The High Priestess is nothing if not deep.

TREE OF LIFE: divine principle, personal development, universal law, inner life, energy flow, ascension. In the RWS tarot, the Tree of Life formation is alluded to by an arrangement of pomegranates. I chose to be more direct and show the traditional Qabalistic Tree of Life symbol. The Tree of Life is an energetic road map of the inner life of humankind, encompassing both the conscious and the unconscious as well as the hidden worlds that lie above and below our everyday consciousness. It consists of 11 energies (collectively called sephirot) connected by 22 pathways, with each path corresponding to a Major Arcana card.

TRIPLE GODDESS SYMBOL: phases, cycles, divine feminine, magic. An ancient symbol that has become downright trendy in modern times, the triple goddess portrays three phases of the moon: waxing, full, and waning. The simplest belief regarding this symbol is that the phases represent the three aspects of womanhood: the Maiden, the Mother, and the Crone. But a richer explanation identifies the three phases as three specific Greek goddesses: Persephone, Demeter, and Hecate. The story goes that Persephone caught the eye of Hades, god of the Underworld, who essentially kidnapped her and took her to his realm. Demeter, Persephone's mother and goddess of the harvest and agriculture, desperately searched everywhere for her daughter and implored Zeus for assistance. Zeus did nothing to help however, so Demeter turned to Hecate, goddess of magic and witchcraft, who aided her in her search. (Girls gotta stick together, am I right?) It was finally decided that Persephone would spend half of the year in the Underworld with Hades and the other half on the surface with her mother. Demeter's sadness when Persephone was away meant nothing would grow until her daughter's return;

this story serves as a metaphor for the cycles of the seasons. Hecate became a companion to Persephone during her time in the Underworld. Interestingly, Hecate is also sometimes referred to as "the Crone goddess," as well as the goddess of the dark side of the moon. There are so many rich layers of symbolism that can be mined from this story alone regarding the High Priestess. There is the symbolism of the divine feminine as represented by the trio of goddesses. There is also Hecate's tie to the Underworld, hinting at the High Priestess's association with mystery and the depths of hidden wisdom to be discovered within our own subconscious.

TWIN PILLARS: sacredness, duality, entrance, knowledge. Both architecturally and symbolically, twin pillars have long represented a gateway or passage into sacred and mysterious places, such as the biblical Temple of Solomon. The contrasting colors of the two pillars symbolize duality between opposing concepts; light and dark, masculine and feminine, heaven and earth, and yes and no (to name a few). In traditional RWS decks, the pillars are each shown with an inscribed letter of Hebrew origin: *B* on the dark pillar for *Boaz* and *J* on the other for *Jachin*. When combined, this translates to "In his strength, he will establish." This model of twin pillars can also be found in Freemason practices.

QUICK TAKES: Trust your inner knowing, be private about your affairs today, work with the energy of the moon, retreat and reflect on a situation, meditate, embrace your divine feminine energy and spiritual professions. Being single can be liberating.

REVERSED: *ignoring your intuition, lies or withheld information, secrets coming to light, menstrual issues.*

3. The Empress

KEYWORDS: abundance, nurturing, femininity, creativity, fertility, motherhood, insecurity, dependence, infertility, creative blocks

ASSOCIATIONS

Astrological: none

Planetary: Venus

Elemental: earth

Symbols

NUMBER THREE: completeness, union, time, divinity. The number three encompasses multiple concepts rooted in a sense of time: past, present, future; birth, life, death; beginning, middle, end. The Empress has a keen sense of the cycles of time due to her deep connection with the natural world. Three also carries a spiritual energy as it is found in multiple religious traditions: the Christian Holy Trinity, the three aspects of the Egyptian sun god, and even the three primary gods of ancient Babylon. Many interpret the Empress of the traditional RWS deck to be pregnant, which means we can also consider one of the simplest meanings of the number three—the love union of two creates three.

CROWN (DIADEM): cycles, divine connection, authority. The diadem the Empress wears houses 12 stars representing both the 12 months of the year and the 12 zodiac signs. She is simultaneously in tune with the earthly cycles of nature as well as connected to the heavens.

HEART-SHAPED SHIELD: love, beauty, sensuality, divine protection. The heart-shaped shield of the Empress bears the symbol of Venus, goddess of love, sex, beauty, and fertility. The form of a shield represents the notion that where there is love, there is also protection. The Romans and Greeks adopted Venus as the goddess of all things sexy, as well as love, fertility, and victory. She was worshipped by the ancient Italians as the goddess of cultivated fields. As the Empress card also depicts wheat, I think we can take all aspects of Venus's identity into account in the meaning of this card. Simply put: cultivate love.

LAUREL WREATH: victory, success, triumph, protection, wish fulfillment, transformation. In Greek mythology, the god Apollo aggressively pursues the nymph Daphne after being struck by one of Eros's arrows. Daphne, having made an oath to celibacy, rejects his advances and flees with him hot on her heels. Her father intervenes on her behalf, turning her into a laurel tree to save her from Apollo's obsession. This little mythological tale makes the laurel wreath the Empress wears symbolic of the transformative energy inherent in her powers of creation. Whether it's a mother creating new life in her womb or an artist creating art, what we generate in this world has the potential to forever change us.

PEARL NECKLACE: love, incorruptibility, wisdom, the planets, lunar energy, femininity, hidden magic. All naughty euphemisms aside, this pearl necklace specifically has seven pearls to represent the seven classical planets (the sun and moon, Mercury, Venus, Mars, Jupiter, and Saturn—the seven heavenly bodies that could be seen by ancient astrologers with the naked eye). This links the Empress to the cosmos as well as the earthly realm, suggesting her powers of creation are on par with the universe itself. I know some pregnant women who have felt as "big as a planet." The Empress takes this concept to the next level. Pearls are also linked to the goddess Venus (and by default, the planet) making the Empress's tie to the divine feminine even stronger.

POMEGRANATE: abundance, fertility, womb, divine feminine, wisdom, death. The lush pomegranate is an apt symbol for the fertile energy of the Empress. In addition to being a symbol of the womb itself, it has also been depicted held in the hands of the Virgin Mary or being fed to Mary by the baby Jesus, such as in Botticelli's painting *Virgin and Child with Angels*, linking it to both the divine feminine and the nurturing aspect of motherhood.

Did you know this delicious fruit inspired one of the most destructive weapons in history? If a pomegranate is allowed to overripen on the tree, it will explode, launching hundreds of seeds in all directions. Each of these seeds holds the potential for new trees and growth. The grenade was invented with a similar construction and was even named for the fruit. (Its name comes from the French word for pomegranate . . . *grenade*.) While the Empress does not dabble in such violent pursuits, she does indicate potent fertile energy on par with the explosive potential of this ripe fruit.

PILLOW: comfort, sensuality. The red color of the pillow represents passion as well as the menstrual cycle.

SCEPTER: power, royalty. The Empress's scepter denotes her sovereignty, in this case over the natural world. Under her rule, everything grows lush and abundant. The orb adorning the top of the scepter mimics the shape of the Earth itself, another indication of her domain.

SIX-POINTED STARS: possibility, faith, protection, heavens. The shape of the stars in the Empress's diadem is also significant. Created from two interlocking triangles (one pointing downward and one pointing upward), it can be considered a visual representation of the phrase "as above, so below." Even in all her lush beauty in the earthly realm, the Empress is still connected to the spiritual realm.

TREE: growth, lushness, potential, sustainability, expansion, ascension, time. The energy of abundance represented by the Empress is mirrored in the expansive growth symbolized by trees.

WATER: life, abundance, movement, ebb and flow, purification, power, depth, intuition. The vertical water of the Empress card is a waterfall. All of the associated meanings of water are amplified in a waterfall. It's hard to picture a waterfall without envisioning the sheer power created by all that water rushing downward. The Empress is a formidable force herself with the innate abundance she brings to the table. Like water, she has the ability to create and nurture life. It is said that dreaming of a waterfall can symbolize the birth of an infant or new idea . . . the Empress is associated with both possibilities. (In many decks, she is portrayed pregnant.) Taking the water symbolism a step further, the downward gush of fluid that occurs when a pregnant woman's "water breaks" just before labor can be seen as a powerful waterfall that ushers in new life.

WHEAT: nourishment, bounty, renewal, rebirth, harvest. Mythologically, wheat is linked to the Greek goddess Demeter. Demeter is sometimes represented as one of the three goddesses that make up the triple goddess symbol. She represents the mother aspect of the Maiden/Mother/Crone trinity. The Empress is often depicted as a pregnant woman, solidifying this mother energy.

A common saying that pairs as perfectly with wheat as bread and butter is "You reap what you sow." The Empress card can be a potent card for creatives; the wheat symbol asks you to consider carefully what creative seeds you're sowing and avoid the temptation to harvest the results of your efforts too soon. (This is particularly poignant with the current trend of using artificial intelligence to create art and card decks. While I'm not passing judgment on whether AI is a valid tool to use in creation, I will say that planting creative seeds with little thought or effort usually results in a tasteless crop.)

QUICK TAKES: Surround yourself with beauty, treat yourself, express yourself artistically, create and nurture through pregnancy or adoption. Get out in nature, revel in self-love, embrace your role as a mother figure. Also suggests issues with a mother figure, a message from a mother spirit, a new idea or business venture. Tap into your femininity, seek a mentor or mentor others, explore holistic remedies. Also alludes to a healthy relationship with a lover.

REVERSED: *creative blocks, suppressing your feminine side, a smothering mother figure, unplanned pregnancy, fertility issues.*

4. The Emperor

KEYWORDS: logic, action, structure, patriarchy, protection, fatherhood, maturity, stubbornness, domineering, recklessness, unfocused

ASSOCIATIONS

Astrological: Aries

Planetary: Mars

Elemental: fire

Symbols

NUMBER FOUR: stability, foundations, organization.

ARMOR: protection, shield, self-preservation, preparation, strength, truth, chivalry, honor, mirroring, boundaries. Fun fact: the metals iron and steel (which armor is typically made of) are governed by the planet Mars, which just so happens to be the governing planet of the Emperor himself. You'll also notice his armor is blue in color. In the Qabalistic Tree of Life, the pillar of mercy is opposite the pillar of severity, and blue is generally the color associated with mercy. The blue armor represents the way the Emperor tempers his severity with mercy . . . the true measure of any good leader.

BEARD: wisdom, experience, maturity, passage of time, communication, enlightenment. The word *pogonotrophos* was used by the ancient Greeks to mean both "bearded man" and "philosopher." In this same way, when we see a white-bearded figure, our minds assume wisdom and knowledge. It's also interesting to note that many cultures believe hair to be a sort of spiritual antennae, aiding us in absorbing cosmic energies. So beyond even mere wisdom, there is a sense of enlightenment that the Emperor represents. Since a beard is located near the mouth, there is also the representation of the power of our words.

CROWN: rulership, authority, divinity. While crowns represent earthly matters such as ruling over a certain domain, they also symbolize our connection to the divine. It's no coincidence that the seventh chakra—which connects us to the cosmos and the divine—is named the "crown chakra."

Crowns are also linked to the mental realm. We can look to the word's etymology for an even deeper mental association. There are several roots to the word *crown*. One is to the ancient Greek word *koronē*, meaning "crow or raven." In Norse mythology, Odin's two ravens, Huginn and Muninn, are often sent out to acquire information. They are understood to be projections of his thoughts and aid him in acquiring more knowledge. (Even their names reinforce this: Huginn means "thought," and Muninn means "memory or mind.") The crown of the authoritative Emperor reminds us to be in full control of our own thoughts, lest they run wild (or in this case, fly).

MOUNTAINS: challenges, obstacles, constancy, perspective. Mountains are prevalent throughout the traditional imagery of the tarot, but their meanings can be diverse. For the Emperor, I believe those mountains are less about challenges and more of a tool in which he can gain perspective from a higher vantage point. With his action-based nature, it is likely he is seeking a higher vantage point in order to methodically strategize his best course of action.

ORB: heaven, cosmos, femininity. Even with all his outward masculine energy, the Emperor is still in perfect balance with his feminine counterpart, the Empress.

RAM: leadership, bravery, strength, power, determination, virility, masculinity, ascension, astrological sign of Aries. The ram is the symbol of the Emperor's ruling astrological sign of Aries. This powerful creature's headbutting talents inspired the ancient medieval weapon known as a battering ram. Used to batter down the gates or walls of a castle, this powerful armament was a game-changer when it came to penetrating well-constructed medieval fortresses. (Goodness, all this penetrating talk definitely reinforces the Emperor's symbolic virility.) The ram suggests it may be time to take a page from the Emperor's playbook and try a more forceful and direct approach to a situation in order to remove obstacles from your path. And while I'm not advocating for violence, a touch of lighthearted aggression is sometimes just the thing. To quote the movie *Princess Bride*, "Have fun storming the castle!"

SCEPTER: power, royalty, masculinity, authority, life, immortality. The Emperor's scepter is unique in that it is topped by an ankh. The ankh is an ancient Egyptian power symbol representing truth, regeneration, and life. As with any symbol that has a rich history of use, there are several meanings associated with the ankh. One that I am partial to that is based on its shape is the union of masculine and feminine. The lower phallic shape can be seen to represent the male anatomy while the upper part takes on the form of the female uterus. This brings us full circle back to the original meaning of "life"—the sexual union of masculine and feminine is what creates literal life. Also, if the shape of this symbol looks vaguely familiar to you, it could be the due to its resemblance to the symbol for the planet Venus, found on the Empress card (the counterpart to the Emperor). Just as Venus is associated with love and beauty, the Emperor rules with both authority and love.

THRONE: authority, power, royal status, elevation. The throne of the Emperor is the perfect reminder to sit comfortably in our full authority.

WATER: emotions, ebb and flow, power, depth, intuition, subconscious. Water is the element of emotions and the subconscious. The water in this card is merely a narrow stream, indicating that while the Emperor may strive for balance, these energies are not naturally his forte. Much less forceful than the waterfall of the Empress, the thin stream also indicates the Emperor is not one to be easily overwhelmed by his emotions.

QUICK TAKES: Assert your personal power, take immediate action, lean on your intellect, use strategic thinking. Indicates a father figure, a business mentor, pushing past obstacles and challenges. Be disciplined with your money; embrace self-discipline.

REVERSED: *someone being bullied, a need for boundaries, out of touch with emotions, abuse of power, a cruel male, a power struggle within a relationship.*

5. The Hierophant

KEYWORDS: law, tradition, religion, authority, ethics, morality, teaching, wholeness, freedom, rebellion, personal beliefs

ASSOCIATIONS

Astrological: Taurus

Planetary: Venus

Elemental: earth

Symbols

NUMBER FIVE: humanity, physicality, expansiveness. Since the Hierophant is all about that religious life, we can take into consideration the religious associations of the number five: In Christianity, there are Five Sacred Wounds that Jesus Christ suffered during the crucifixion, the book of Psalms is arranged into five books, and the Torah contains the Five Books of Moses. The Greeks considered the pentagram (a five-pointed star) a perfect symbol, representing the four elements plus the fifth element of spirit that brings a sense of unity to all elements.

BLACK AND WHITE CHECKERED CLOTH: opposing forces, duality, extremes, balance. You may have thought Vans® was the OG when it comes to black and white checkers, but the Hierophant has been sporting that signature pattern for eons. This is one of many visual representations on this card of the union of opposites or a joining of the earthly and heavenly principles.

HAND GESTURE: blessing, mystery. The hand gesture seen in the Hierophant is a common one used by the pope and other religious figures, typically as a blessing. The fingers also point heavenward, adding to the spiritual significance. The right hand is the one making the gesture, which is considered the hand that gives energy—as opposed to the left hand which receives energy. Other interpretations suggest the meaning of this gesture translates to "all you see is not all that there is." But the configuration of the fingers is also very similar to a mudra called *kapithaka* used in Indian dance.

KEY: mysteries, knowledge, wisdom. The keys on this card represent the keys to the "kingdom of Heaven," making the Hierophant a sort of intermediary between humanity and God, or the deeper concept of a key being the tool to unlock knowledge. There are also some references to the keys linking the Hierophant to Hades. Hades is the Greek god of the Underworld, who was the holder of a symbolic set of keys—one to heaven and one to hell. One of the Hierophant's main attributes is that of wholeness. Wholeness can imply a balancing of dichotomies. Just as you can't have light without dark, you conceptually can't have heaven without hell. The keys are also colored blue and reddish-orange. In Qabalah, blue is the color of mercy, while red is the color of severity. The Hierophant is a figure that leans more toward stern severity with a dash of mercy sprinkled in; hence, the red key is *over* the blue key (and the background of the card as a whole is red).

LILY: purity, virtue, innocence, knowledge, feminine principle, rebirth. The Hierophant's counterpart is the High Priestess, who is symbolically linked to the Virgin Mary. In Christianity, the white lily is associated with the Virgin Mary. I personally think this association helps to balance the otherwise dominantly masculine energy of the pope-like Hierophant. (Ever heard the expression "it needs a woman's touch"?) One of the key qualities attributed to the Hierophant card is "wholeness," and we can only be truly whole on a spiritual level when we honor and balance our own divine feminine and masculine energies. Another feminine tie to lilies is the story of the Greek goddess Hera. After her cad of a husband, Zeus, had an affair with a mortal woman that resulted in the birth of Hercules, he tried to sneak Hercules into Hera's breastfeeding rotation with her other children in the hopes this would make Hercules more powerful. Infuriated upon discovering this, Hera pushed the baby Hercules off her breast, spouting a fountain of milk onto the ground, which turned into . . . you guessed it . . . lilies! Hence, the lily can also be seen as a symbol of the spiritual nourishment that the Hierophant offers.

NAIL: joining, union. Just as a nail joins two things together, the energy of the Hierophant serves to "join" humanity to God or the heavens. In more modern or nonreligious terms, this can be seen as a metaphor for enlightenment.

PALLIUM: The white thing that looks a bit like a fancy tie is a symbol of the office held by the pope, archbishops, and some bishops in the Catholic Church. The white color represents purity of thought, and the unequal-armed crosses symbolize the bridge between divine knowledge and humanity. The fact that a pallium is made of white wool simultaneously represents the role of the good shepherd leading the flock (or congregation) as well as the lamb (Christ) that was sacrificed to save humanity from sin.

PILLARS: structure, support, strength, portal, knowledge, illusion, spiritual ascension, grandiosity. Twin columns or pillars in the tarot are generally representative of a gateway to knowledge. But whereas the twin pillars of the High Priestess are traditionally depicted connected with a veil, the Hierophant's pillars are open in the middle, representing a more accessible and direct knowledge versus the mysterious inner wisdom of the High Priestess.

ROSE: passion, vitality, enlightenment, secret wisdom, unfolding, illumination, masculine principle. In alchemy, there is an allegory featuring a red king and a white queen. Sometime referred to as the "chemical marriage," their union represents the process of uniting opposites to create a greater product of that union. Here, the red rose and the white lily work together to symbolically recreate this allegory, alluding to the spiritual wholeness signaled by the Hierophant.

SCEPTER: power, royalty, masculinity, authority. Also known as the papal cross, this traditional symbol of the office of the pope has a triple cross formation to represent the three roles of the pope as lawgiver, judge, and teacher. But another perspective can be found in the Kundalini tradition. There is an illustration in the alchemical text *Speculum Veritatis* (which just so happens to be housed in the Vatican's library) that depicts the "alchemical oven" of the pelvis and spine as well as a triangle shape with three arrows (the triangle is the alchemical symbol of fire), indicating that body, thinking, and feeling have been purified by the Kundalini fire of the spine. We see this same visual metaphor represented in the papal scepter with the long shaft representing the spine and the three crosses at the top forming a triangular shape.

THREE-TIERED CROWN: Known historically as the papal tiara or by the Latin word *triregnum*, papal tiaras were worn by all popes starting with Pope Clement V continuing up to Pope Paul VI (crowned in 1963). The intended symbolism is widely disputed but two of the simpler interpretations I prefer are: The threefold nature of Christ as priest, prophet, and King, and the pope's three roles as lawgiver, judge, and teacher. It is also said to represent the three worlds over which the Hierophant rules: the conscious, the subconscious, and the superconscious.

VAV (ו): The translation of this Hebrew letter is "nail." Interestingly, it is also equivalent to the conjunction "and" in English, which joins nouns together in a sentence, much like a nail joins two objects together. This same energy of joining is seen throughout the symbols on the Hierophant where dualities are joined to create a sense of wholeness.

QUICK TAKES: Spiritual completeness. The wisdom you seek comes from within, the power of ritual, a leadership role, a spiritual mentor, a teacher figure or a calling to teach—"as you teach, so will you learn"—a reminder to have faith in yourself, create your own traditions, rebel against societal norms. Embrace healthy skepticism.

REVERSED: *inflexibility or intolerance toward others, disrespect for authority, the dark side of organized religion, abuse of power in religion, trouble with an authority figure.*

6. The Lovers

KEYWORDS: love, sexuality, attraction, relationships, choices, self-love, imbalance, disharmony, disconnection, indecision

ASSOCIATIONS

Astrological: Gemini

Planetary: Mercury

Elemental: air

Symbols

NUMBER SIX: harmony, union, integration. One of the shapes based on the number six is a hexagon. A beautiful illustration of the harmony six brings are the hexagonal shapes found in a beehive: bees work together in perfect harmony and union to create something greater than themselves. Another lovely visual alluded to by the shape of the number six is the human eye—when we see with love, we see with divine clarity.

ANGEL: blessings, love, divinity, protection, messages. The angel represented in the Lovers card is Archangel Raphael, whose name means "God heals." I absolutely adore Raphael's energy! He can be called upon to assist us with love and relationships as well as healing on all levels. He is also known as the angel of air, the element associated with the Lovers card. In Qabalah, mercy is represented by the color blue and severity is represented by the color red. In the RWS tarot, the angel is typically depicted wearing a purple shawl—the perfect balance of blue and red when mixed. Consider this a nudge from Archangel Raphael to strive for balance in our own relationships.

APPLE: knowledge, temptation, nourishment. Known as the Tree of the Knowledge of Good and Evil (and usually depicted in art as an apple tree), it is famous in the story of Adam and Eve for bearing the forbidden fruit that would bring consciousness and awareness to them after being ingested. The anatomy of an apple is also telling—when sliced open, the arrangement of the seeds forms a pentagram, a symbol associated with magic (and magic is a by-product of secret knowledge).

On the Lovers card, the apples are a literal representation of the forbidden fruit from the Tree of the Knowledge of Good and Evil . . . you know, all that tired old biblical drama from the Garden of Eden? It turns out that story might have a deeper meaning than you might have realized. See, what happened when Adam and Eve partook of that fruit was more profound than just the loss of innocence for humankind. They gained awareness—or in other words, consciousness. It was in that moment that they acquired freedom of choice for humankind. This metaphor is the chef's kiss of perfection for the Lovers card because besides being ripe with the energy of gushy, swoony, sappy, sexy love, the Lovers card is also known as . . . (wait for it) . . . the card of CHOICE!

In ancient Greece, the apple tree was referred to as the Tree of Love and was associated with Aphrodite (who just happens to be the goddess of love. Seeing a pattern yet?). The myth for this one is a long one, so I'll just give you the CliffNotes. (But it's a good one, so go read it sometime.) Aphrodite got the designation of goddess of love because Eris, the goddess of discord, threw down a golden apple at a wedding. Upon the apple was inscribed, "to the fairest one." Hera, Athena, and Aphrodite all thought themselves to be the bomb dot com and applied for the position. Not wanting to upset anyone, Zeus decreed that the human Paris would determine the winner, and he (obviously) chose Aphrodite. Ahem . . . he made a CHOICE.

And it was a doozy because it basically started the Trojan War. (You know, *that* old chestnut.) From this tale, we can take the discord to represent the inevitable friction and struggles that can be inherent in a long-term relationship. We can also take a warning from this myth to always choose carefully.

CLOUDS: element of air, thoughts, constancy of change, hidden information, lack of clarity, silver linings, dreams, divinity. The psychological phenomenon of seeing objects in clouds is called pareidolia. (There's your trivia word for the day.) The formations they make are beautifully diverse, some of which humans have even attempted to categorize and name. For example, a type of cloud called a mammatus cloud was named for its uncanny resemblance to . . . well, boobs. Just as two people can gaze at the same cloud and see two completely different things, they may also see different things in the same situation. As the Lovers card is often about relationships, the cloud reminds us to strive to see things from our partner's perspective.

FIRE TREE: passion, desire. The 12 flames emanating from the tree (the Tree of Life) are indicative of the 12 signs of the zodiac. This may be a wild tangent to take, but I can't help but think of the prescribed burns set intentionally in certain forest areas. Fire is often seen as a purely destructive force, but scientists have discovered that some forest fires actually clear the underbrush and rejuvenate the soil, allowing heartier regrowth than before. As the Lovers card is the "card of choice," this analogy beautifully illustrates the power and potential that lie in making intentional (although at times difficult) choices for our lives.

HEART: love, romance, sexuality, consciousness, soul. While there are no blatant heart symbols on the RWS Lovers card, I chose to include one as a visual cue to help you instantly home in on the energy of this card. Hearts are unmistakable icons of all things associated with love. As the Lovers is also the "card of choice," it also serves to drive home the message to make a heart-centered choice.

MOUNTAIN: aspiration, courage, challenges, obstacles, retreat, perspective, solitude, ascension. In the first edition of *Tarot Disassembled,* I depicted this as a volcano. As with anything in tarot, there are several schools of thought about it and, personally, I'm still on the fence. The potential energy of the Lovers card definitely vibes at times with the volatility of a volcano. But it is equally conducive to the symbolic energy of a mountain. As this is a card of both intimate relationships and choices, the mountain is the perfect symbol for the challenges and obstacles that can arise on the path to achieving a "higher love" or as a consequence to the choices we make. I also decided to introduce the color purple into the palette this time around. In Qabalah, mercy is represented by the color blue and severity by the color red. When purple is in the picture, it indicates a perfect balance between those two concepts—something we should all strive for in our relationships.

SNAKE: renewal, rebirth, temptation, fertility, earthly realm, sexuality, evil, immortality. Not all snakes are poisonous, though that is a quality that many associate with snakes. Any of the dangerous varieties out there are actually best described as "venomous." A creature is considered poisonous when touching or eating it makes you sick. A creature is considered venomous when being bitten or stung by it makes you sick. The distinction is that biting or stinging is an intentional act on the part of the snake. Imagine you're enjoying a peaceful walk in the woods when suddenly you notice your next step is about to be on top of a coiled snake. There's a high probability in this scenario that you will be bitten. Sucks, right? But think of it from the perspective of the snake. There you are, just minding your business and chilling in the grass when a big ol' shoe looms over you, threatening to step on you. You use the weapon nature gave you and strike to defend. When we experience discord in relationships, it's easy to make the other person out to be a villain, when the reality is they are likely just reacting defensively in an effort to protect their emotions. The snake reminds us that the true poison in a relationship is when one or both parties cling to the need to be right.

SUN: life force, joy, optimism, vitality, illumination, masculine principle. Most would agree that being in love can feel like the warmth of the sun shining down on you, infusing your cells (and loins) with vitality and joy. But a much deeper meaning might be attributed to the sun symbol on this card. In the Qabalistic Tree of Life diagram, Kether (or Keter) is the topmost sephirah, shining infinite light down and activating all other sephirot. Also known as the "crown sephirah," it is linked to the divine will of the Creator. It's only a small hop, skip, and a jump from here to infer that it was God's will that humans be given the gift of consciousness and free will in the Garden of Eden.

TRIANGLE: In the RWS Lovers card, there is no obvious triangle depicted; rather one is implied by the direction of the gazes among the figures: the man looks to the woman, who looks up to the angel, who looks down upon them both. This triad represents the evolution from physical desire to emotional needs to spiritual concerns. It is also a nod to the conscious, subconscious, and superconscious triad alluded to in other cards.

QUICK TAKES: New love, marriage on the horizon, a new sexual partner, a union of opposites, a relationship with a solid foundation, make a heart-guided choice, a big decision to be made. Love is on its way, or a platonic partnership. Nurture your own self-love, explore your sexuality, discover your kink.

REVERSED: *imbalance in a relationship, beware of snakes, impulsive choices, lust without connection, a cheating partner, divorce or a breakup, refusing to make a choice.*

7. The Chariot

KEYWORDS: success, self-discipline, ambition, action, willpower, movement, opposition, directionless, powerless, stagnation

ASSOCIATIONS

Astrological: Cancer

Planetary: moon

Elemental: water

Symbols

NUMBER SEVEN: awakening, growth, wisdom, planning, completeness. I could write an entire book about the number seven and its many associations. On a simply whimsical note, I can't help but think of the seven wonders of the ancient world and how they would have made up a traveler's ultimate bucket list. After all, one of the most literal interpretations of the Chariot can be an indication that travel is in the cards.

ARMOR: protection, shield, self-preservation, preparation, strength, truth, chivalry, honor, mirroring, boundaries. The charioteer's armor is unique in that it is emblazoned with a square on the chest plate. The square is a symbol for the element of earth, and indicates being grounded in the material world in our endeavors. As the Chariot is generally considered a positive card, we can usually infer that we are safe moving forward with our plans when it appears in a reading. With this card, I also think the symbolic meaning of preparation is fitting here. Things are bound to move fast when the Chariot is in play—it's best to be prepared for anything.

If you'll allow me a brief nerd-out, my favorite superhero (or at least one of my top three) is Tony Stark, better known as Iron Man. One of the things I love about Iron Man (besides his snarky comebacks) is that, unlike many superheroes in the comic book genre, he is a mere mortal like the rest of us. His impressive suits of armor seemingly transform him into a force to be reckoned with. But when it comes down to it, the armor is merely an extension of him. Created using his supreme intellect and worn with inarguable bravery that already resides within him, the armor is nothing more than a manifestation of some of his most extraordinary qualities. The armor of the charioteer reminds us that in order make forward progress in life, we must acknowledge the power and excellence that already exists within us.

BELT: time, zodiac, elliptical energy. The zodiac-adorned belt of the charioteer represents the vastness of the universe and the passage of time. The symbol found front and center on the belt is the sign of Cancer, which is associated with the Chariot card as a whole. Cancer is connected to the infinite wisdom of the universe and teaches us that our most profound guiding force on our journey is intuition. The elliptical shape of the belt also mimics the Earth's elliptical orbit around the sun, and therefore the passage of time.

CANOPY: divinity, celestial, heavens, protection. Covered in six-pointed stars, the canopy represents our connection to the heavens as well as our own divine nature.

CROWN: elevation, mastery, power, authority, intellect, divinity. We all know that crowns denote a certain sense of royalty and power. But you don't need to be a literal king or queen to vibe with this prevalent symbol. Crowns represent authority or mastery over a particular domain. That could look like mastery over our mental domain when we control what thoughts we allow to stick around. Or it could be mastery of our emotional domain when we are in flow with a healthy range of balanced emotions. Mastery over these domains is what allows us to take the reins and steer our chariot with authority.

CUBE: initiation, dominion, spiritual development, spiritual evolution. The Cube of Space is a three-dimensional structure that contains a dizzyingly complex system intended to represent varying degrees or grades of spiritual development. It also encompasses the 22 Major Arcana cards of tarot in its sugar cube-like dimensionality. This shape is definitely deep dive-worthy and, in my opinion, sets this charioteer on a path to spiritual ascension of the highest degree.

DOUBLE-TIPPED WAND: divine inspiration, spiritual wisdom, will, conduit, harmony, perfect union, balance. Just as the Magician uses the double-tipped wand to focus their intention, so does the charioteer. In the RWS tarot, the charioteer holds no reins, only the wand, making a profound statement about the power of channeling their focus and willpower to forcefully direct their intent. The charioteer works a sort of magic by manifesting their desires through doggedly staying on their path. As the famous mystic Éliphas Lévi said, "All magic is in the will."

EIGHT-POINTED STAR: hope, guidance, balance. There are a ton of varied meanings for the eight-pointed star that exist throughout different cultures. One that I feel beautifully corresponds to the energy of the Chariot is from the Wiccan religion. The Wiccan Wheel of the Year is commonly represented as a circle containing an eight-pointed star. Each point on the star represents a Sabbat, or major Wiccan holiday. Wiccans view this system of holidays as a whole, with each one being influenced by what has come before as well as what comes next, a fitting representation of the life movement implied by the Chariot.

The eight-pointed star is also an emblem of the ancient Babylonian goddess Ishtar. Ishtar is associated with the planet Venus. Venus appears to us from Earth as the most prominent, brightest star in the sky at dawn. Some have even speculated that the famed Star of

Bethlehem in the Bible that guided the wise men was, in fact, Venus. As the Chariot is a card of powerful forward movement, the eight-pointed star suggests we are being divinely guided on this path.

LAUREL WREATH: victory, success, triumph, protection, wish fulfillment. In ancient Greece, the laurel tree was dedicated to the god Apollo, who just so happens to be one of the most famous charioteers of lore. His daily godly tasks included hitching four horses to his golden chariot in order to pull the sun across the sky. Ancient Romans believed that lightning would not strike a laurel tree, prompting the Emperor Tiberius to wear a laurel wreath at all times for protection. In magical traditions, laurel is also believed to ward off evil spirits. How does this apply to the energy of the Chariot? In addition to its more obvious properties of victory and success, I believe laurel symbolizes that when we intentionally take the reins and forge our own path, we are divinely protected.

MALLET: self-control, accomplishment, skill, labor. In Freemasonry, the mallet holds special significance as the first tool the apprentice learns. It is also the symbolic tool of the highest office—Master Mason. This beautifully illustrates the movement the Chariot symbolizes from one checkpoint to another and the potential for extreme success when we fully commit ourselves to our goals and work hard.

MOON: intuition, cycles, emotions, divine feminine, subconscious. The moon rules the astrological sign of Cancer, the sign associated with the Chariot. For all of the physicality and force of will of the charioteer, the moon reminds us that to be fully in control of our path we must also strive to understand our emotions. There are also multiple deities associated with the moon that just so happen to drive a chariot. Selene, the Greek goddess of the moon, was said to drive a chariot across sky, providing the night with light. The Norse god Mani similarly pulled the moon across the sky with a chariot.

SIX-POINTED STAR: balance, possibility, faith, protection, heavens. A universal symbol with a varied history of usage, the six-pointed star is created from two interlocking triangles—one pointing downward and one pointing upward—a visual representation of the phrase "as above, so below." The Freemasons also saw the two triangles as representative of the perfect balance between the feminine principle (downward-pointing triangle) and the masculine principle (upward-pointing triangle).

Also known as the Star of David, one of the oldest known appearances of the six-pointed star is in the Leningrad Codex, the oldest complete copy of the Hebrew Bible dating back to 1008. In 1897, the Star of David became officially associated with Judaism when it was chosen as the symbol to appear on the flag at the First Zionist Congress in 1897 (which later became the flag for the State of Israel). One of the meanings attributed to this star is that God rules over the universe and protects us from all six directions: north, south, east, west, up, and down with the middle (the hexagram) representing the spiritual dimension. Historically, this led the six-pointed star to be considered a symbol of protection, with many believing that wearing one in the form of jewelry or adorning a structure with one would invoke God's protection. Kabbalists saw the symbol as a protection against evil spirits.

In modern times this symbol is most visually well-known for its association with Judaism, although it has also been used historically by other religions. In Christianity it's referred to as the "Star of Creation"—the six points are thought to represent the six days of the Creation as well as the six properties of God: power, wisdom, majesty, love, mercy, and justice. It has also been found in the Buddhist Tibetan Book of the Dead and is considered an important symbol in Hinduism to represent divine union.

The takeaway of all this rich symbology for the Chariot is that we are divinely protected on our life's journey when we take the reins and balance our own opposing forces.

SPHINX: mysteries, sacred wisdom, divinity, riddles, guardianship, duality, nobility, threshold. The dual sphinxes of the Chariot card are contrasting colors, indicating opposing forces that need to be reined in and controlled through sheer force of will in order to reach a common destination. The white one represents the sun, the masculine principle, and the conscious. The black one represents the moon, the feminine principle, and the unconscious. Together they symbolize the necessary balancing of energies to find one's path.

TRAGEDY/COMEDY MASKS: masks, roles, emotions. Representing the dichotomous emotions of happiness and sadness, the masks serve to remind us to be aware of our emotions when charging forward on our quest. On a deeper level, they also beckon us to consider what masks we wear when striving for success. Are we coming from a place of authenticity? Or are we taking on a role simply to get to where we want in life?

WATER: emotions, life, abundance, movement, ebb and flow, power, depth, intuition, subconscious. The water in the Chariot card reminds us that we are bound to experience a multitude of emotions as we take action toward our goals, but not to let them dominate the situation. A Chariot can be difficult to steer through a flooded road but a few puddles won't stop our momentum. For the charioteer, emotions and subconscious impulses are just a few of the things that will need to be reined in at times to achieve success. Water also indicates that even when we take the reins to steer the situation, it's important to remain flexible and go with the flow" when needed.

WHEEL: movement, progress.

WINGED SUN: divinity, royalty, power, ascension, goodness, swiftness. The winged sun has been used as a symbol by a multitude of ancient cultures including Egypt, as well as modern orders such as the Freemasons. Associated with the Egyptian god Horus, when the sun is used as a hieroglyph it means "to become—to be—to create." This is perfect—we can almost imagine the Chariot card asking us, "What do you want to become? What do you want to create? Good. Now how do you get there?"

Another association I find particularly relevant is with the Greek god Hermes. The winged sun is traditionally shown adorning the top of Hermes's staff. Among other things, Hermes is known as the god of travel and roads. Thanks to his fancy-schmancy winged sandals, he was also hailed as the fastest of the gods. As the RWS tarot is replete with both Egyptian and Freemasonry symbolism, it's possible that Waite and Smith primarily included the winged sun due to its meanings from those orders. But I can't help but think the quick-moving energy of the Chariot pairs perfectly with the energy of good ol' Hermes.

Wondering why the winged sun seems vaguely familiar, even in modern times? Well, there is one last visual reference to add to this list: the Golden Snitch made famous in the Harry Potter books. (Perhaps you've heard of him?) This one might be a stretch, but I personally believe that the best symbols reverberate throughout history long after their origins. And here we again have an example that ties beautifully to the Chariot: Harry's dogged pursuit of the Golden Snitch exemplifies the Chariot's qualities of determination, action, movement, and ultimately, success!

QUICK TAKES: Take action, overcome challenges. Victory. Things are moving full speed ahead. A need for discipline and willpower. You're in the driver's seat, pushing past obstacles, involved in a successful project. Follow through, boldly express yourself. Expect upcoming travel, a road trip, a new car.

REVERSED: *letting someone else steer, change of direction, lack of motivation, delay of plans, canceled trip, automotive problems.*

8. Strength

KEYWORDS: strength, bravery, confidence,self-control, power, patience, balance, compassion, self-doubt, cowardice

ASSOCIATIONS

Astrological: Leo

Planetary: sun

Elemental: fire

Symbols

NUMBER EIGHT: infinity, wisdom, confidence.

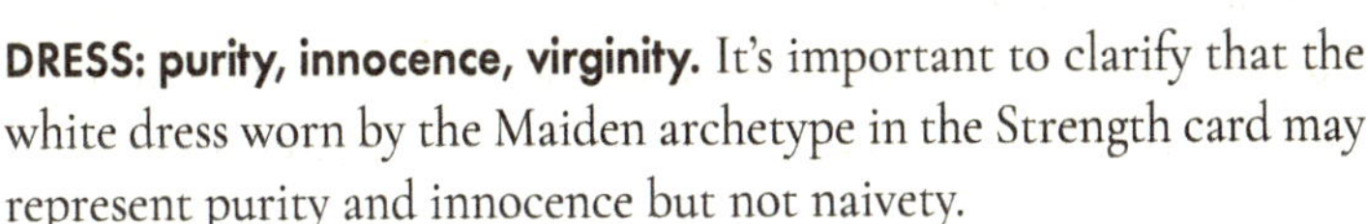

DRESS: purity, innocence, virginity. It's important to clarify that the white dress worn by the Maiden archetype in the Strength card may represent purity and innocence but not naivety.

FLORAL WREATH: infinity, celebration, festivity, victory, honor. The floral wreath is closely linked to the ancient Roman celebration known as Floralia. Floralia was a springtime festival held in honor of the Roman goddess of flowers, Flora, during which festivalgoers would wear wreaths of flowers in their hair and party hard for six straight days. Floralia was known to be quite the pleasure-fest and included performances of lewd self-display by partygoers who would shed their clothes when the mood struck them. On the flip side of Flora's legacy is a little tale of a magical flower she gifted the goddess Juno in order to aid her in the virgin birth of Mars. This duality is present in the Strength card as well. The taming of the lion by the innocent, virginal character is a deeper metaphor for keeping our more primal nature in check.

GREEN LANDSCAPE: fertility, abundance, growth.

LEMNISCATE (INFINITY SYMBOL): infinity, eternity, perpetual motion, limitlessness, balance. The presence of the lemniscate in the Strength card is a reminder that you have a limitless reserve of spiritual strength within you ready to access when the going gets tough. My favorite phrase to describe this is "indomitable spirit." The lemniscate also indicates a need for balancing energies. The Strength card is not about brute strength, so there may be a need to temper strength of will with a dash of self-control.

LION: strength, courage, instinct, primal, ferocity, desire, passion, astrological sign of Leo, solar energy. In addition to representing sheer strength and courage, the lion signifies our own primal nature, which we must keep in check. It is also associated with the zodiacal Leo, the ruling sign of this card. Leos are the ultimate fire signs in the zodiac. A link also exists between lions and the Greek god of the sun, Apollo, called the Terrace of the Lions. On the Greek island of Delos, a series of lion sculptures was erected dedicated to Apollo by the people of Naxos around 600 BCE. This is yet another reason lions are considered symbols of solar and fire energy. The lion symbol represents primal energy. Just like our own primal nature, fire must be carefully controlled so that it does not destroy everything around us.

A lion's roar can be heard for over five miles, making it the loudest roar of all the big cats. When the Strength card appears for you, the lion may be encouraging you to find your own strength using the power of your own voice—let 'em hear you roar!

MOUNTAINS: aspiration, courage, challenges, obstacles. The mountains of the Strength card are small in size compared to other cards. This suggests that there will always be challenges to overcome, but when we approach our struggles confident in our own inner strength, they will always feel less daunting.

ROSE: passion, vitality, transformation, masculine principle.

QUICK TAKES: Inner strength. Balance strength with patience and calm, quiet persuasion, overcome fears and doubts, tame your animal nature, approach a situation with love and compassion. Indicates a relationship with a Leo, a charity, or volunteer work, recovery from illness or injury, adopting a new pet, shadow work.

REVERSAL: *reacting without thinking, a need to restore your energy levels, explosive anger, violence or oppression in a relationship.*

9. The Hermit

KEYWORDS: solitude, wisdom, introspection, self-examination, enlightenment, guidance, meditation, loneliness, isolation, withdrawal

ASSOCIATIONS

Astrological: Virgo

Planetary: Mercury

Elemental: earth

Symbols

NUMBER NINE: completion, achievement, fulfillment.

BEARD: wisdom, experience, maturity, passage of time, enlightenment, isolation. Many cultures believe hair to be a sort of spiritual antennae, aiding us in absorbing cosmic energies. This concept is perfectly suited for the Hermit who is on a solo quest for spiritual enlightenment. Another layer of symbolic meaning we can attribute to the Hermit's beard is that of isolation: the Hermit has intentionally withdrawn from society (at least temporarily) and therefore has no need to concern himself with silly things like grooming. Who needs to look good—or smell good for that matter—when you're getting your enlightenment on after all?

HOODED CLOAK: knowledge, deserving, earned, cloaking. The hooded cloak the Hermit traditionally wears is similar to the hooded robe of a monk. The concept of a monk can be found in multiple religious traditions, and in many cases, the humble robe is something that must be earned. The "hood of knowledge" is worn by the few that are willing to cloak themselves from the world, just as the Hermit isolates on that icy mountaintop in his quest for higher knowledge.

ICY MOUNTAIN: solitude, challenges, obstacles, ascension. The snowy, icy mountains found in the Hermit card indicate they are in a place of solitude, far from the populated civilizations of humankind. The Hermit's choice of locale is intentional: they have deliberately chosen an isolated, barren land for the purpose of uninterrupted introspection. The mountain also represents the spiritual ascension that is taking place as the Hermit isolates to find greater understanding.

LANTERN: illumination, discovery, knowledge, truth, hope. Sometimes referred to as the Lamp of Truth, the Hermit's lantern symbolizes their quest for self-discovery and truth. The lantern reminds us that a true seeker of truth doesn't shy away from shining a light on the creepy-crawlies that hide in the dark. Shine a light on the darker corners of your being, and you might find that what lives there isn't so icky after all.

The phrase *to shine a light* on something means to discover the truth within a situation. I also feel like the lantern adds a positive vibe to this card's energy, representing that there is always hope to be found, even in our darker moments.

SIX-POINTED STAR: balance, possibility, faith, protection, heavens. This star is formed from two interlocking triangles representing a perfect balance between the feminine principle of the downward-pointing triangle and the masculine principle of the upward-pointing triangle. The wisdom the Hermit finds in solitude grants them the understanding that, from a divine perspective, we are all equal and all connected. In Judaism, the six-pointed star (known as the Star of David) is considered an emblem of protection from God, suggesting that we are divinely protected on our inner quest.

STAFF: support, guidance, authority, leadership, pilgrimage, solitude, conduit, magic, healing. The use of a staff dates back to ancient times when a shepherd would employ one to guide their flock of sheep. Though the Hermit has no flock, their solo quest for wisdom will make them a worthy leader when they are ready to reenter the world. The staff is also a common accessory for pilgrims and saints, symbolizing the journey of self-discovery that the Hermit is on. Though different from the double-tipped wand of the Magician, the similarly shaped staff of the Hermit still alludes to a conduit or connection between the spiritual realms and the earthly realms.

STARBURST: light, hope, spiritual enlightenment. Just as the lantern offers light in the darkness, this starburst of light represents the illumination and hope to be found when we seek higher understanding of our own personal truths.

QUICK TAKES: Seek answers within; there is a need for some alone time. Establish a meditation practice, home study, or take virtual classes; take a break, solo retreat, or travel. Avoid social media, seek therapy or counseling, seek advice from a wiser or more mature person, work from home, hike or climb mountains. Celibacy.

REVERSAL: *too much isolation, agoraphobia, loneliness within a relationship, taking a time-out from a relationship, too much focus on materialistic things, a need to put more time and effort into friendships and relationships, dark night of the soul.*

10. Wheel of Fortune

KEYWORDS: change, cycles, karma, destiny, good fortune, turning point, resistance to change, bad luck, misfortune, delays

ASSOCIATIONS

Astrological: none

Planetary: Jupiter

Elemental: fire

Symbols

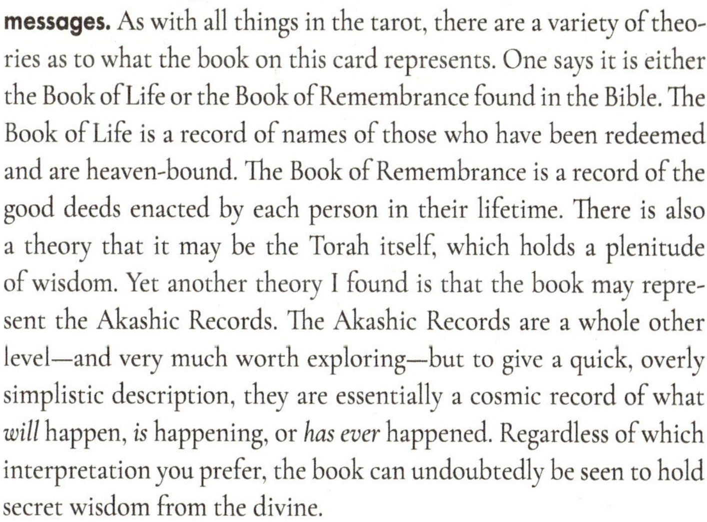

BOOK: knowledge, wisdom, divine messages. As with all things in the tarot, there are a variety of theories as to what the book on this card represents. One says it is either the Book of Life or the Book of Remembrance found in the Bible. The Book of Life is a record of names of those who have been redeemed and are heaven-bound. The Book of Remembrance is a record of the good deeds enacted by each person in their lifetime. There is also a theory that it may be the Torah itself, which holds a plenitude of wisdom. Yet another theory I found is that the book may represent the Akashic Records. The Akashic Records are a whole other level—and very much worth exploring—but to give a quick, overly simplistic description, they are essentially a cosmic record of what *will* happen, *is* happening, or *has ever* happened. Regardless of which interpretation you prefer, the book can undoubtedly be seen to hold secret wisdom from the divine.

CLOUDS: element of air, thoughts, constancy of change, silver linings, dreams, divinity. The symbolic energy of the clouds on the Wheel of

Fortune card is best summed up by this quote by Paulo Coelho: "Don't forget—beautiful sunsets need cloudy skies." With the ups and downs indicated by this card, the cloud is an important reminder that to truly appreciate the beautiful moments, we must also experience the more difficult ones.

SET: chaos, disorder, storms, warfare. That phallic-nosed creature in the bottom left corner is the subject of much debate in the tarot community. Some say it is the Egyptian god Anubis. Others say it is the god Set (or Seth). In the first edition of this deck, I portrayed him as Anubis. But a good friend pointed out that it is actually likely Set, and I honestly think that is much more fitting. Set and Anubis are intricately intertwined in the Egyptian pantheon: Anubis is generally considered the son of Set. Anubis is the god of the afterlife, while Set is the god of chaos, disorder, storms, and warfare. And one could argue the Wheel of Fortune is all about this chaotic life. At its core, the wheel represents the old adage, "Sometimes you're up, sometimes you're down." The universe runs on chaos, and the Wheel of Fortune embodies the sudden shifts and changes that occur in our life that are completely out of our control. With Set also being the god of storms, you can easily make a connection between the sudden change the Wheel of Fortune brings and the sudden occurrence of storms that can wreak complete havoc. You could say there is a balanced structure that exists within chaos. Just as change is the one constant in this world, there is order within the disorder. If you feel you are currently on the chaotic side of the turn of the wheel, take heart. Divine order tells us you'll be back on the calm side before too long.

SNAKE: renewal, rebirth, earthly realm, evil, immortality. The snake here is representative of Typhon, son of the Greek gods Gaea (earth) and Tartarus (the netherworld). Typhon was considered monstrous and evil and symbolizes the downward descent from our divine spiritual form to our more carnal, earthly form. I also believe the symbolic meanings of renewal and rebirth apply here as well. The beauty of the wheel is that it is always turning, so while the snake may symbolize descent, it also symbolizes the opportunity to shed your skin (all that no longer serves you) and emerge renewed as the wheel brings you upward toward spiritual enlightenment once more.

SPHINX: mysteries, sacred wisdom, divinity, riddles, guardianship, duality, nobility, threshold. The sphinx is a complex and mysterious symbol. In the simplest terms, the sphinx in the Wheel of Fortune represents the mystery that lies in the unknowns of what will come next on your path as the wheel turns. It also represents what wisdom you might gain from progressing through multiple revolutions of the wheel.

SWORD: element of air, intellect, power, discernment, decisiveness, truth, impartiality, purification, finality.

TETRAMORPH (ANGEL+EAGLE+LION+BULL): A tetramorph is a composite of four symbols that act together to operate as one collective symbol. In this case, the angel, eagle, lion, and bull combine to create a tetramorph. In Christian tradition, these four are associated with the four evangelists, Matthew, Mark, Luke, and John. Another interpretation of this grouping associates each symbol with an archangel and astrological sign (specifically, the four fixed zodiac signs for those in the know astrologically). They also represent the four elements and corresponding four suits of the tarot. So taking all that into consideration, we get the following correspondences for the symbols: Lion—apostle Mark, Archangel Michael, Leo, element of fire, and suit of Wands; Eagle—apostle John, Archangel Gabriel, Scorpio, element of water, and suit of Cups; Bull—apostle Luke, Archangel Uriel, Taurus, element of earth, and suit of Pentacles; Angel (or human)—apostle Matthew, Archangel Raphael, Aquarius, element of air, and suit of Swords. There's a lot to unpack here, but let's just say this card is deep.

WHEEL: cycles, movement, revolution, progress. The wheel is the headlining star of this card and at the core of its meaning. The cyclical movement of the wheel is an allegory for our lives: sometimes we're up; sometimes we're down. Sometimes we're on top, riding high on life's joyful events; sometimes we're on the bottom, experiencing the tougher stuff life has to offer. One thing holds true—the wheel never stops turning.

The wheel is emblazoned with a series of letters and symbols. Found on the inner part of the wheel are the alchemical symbols mercury (☿), sulfur (🜍), water (🜄), and salt (🜔), corresponding to the four elements air, fire, water, and earth. The four Hebrew letters at the end of the spokes combine to form the Hebrew name for God: *Yod Heh Vav Heh.* Last, we have the letters *TARO*, which just so happen to be the same letters inscribed on the scroll of the High Priestess. To recap the various anagrams of these four letters: *tora* is the Hebrew word for "direction and instruction," *rota* is Latin for "wheel," *taro* is a shortened form of "tarot," *orat* has Latin origins meaning "to speak" (or teach), and *ator* can be seen as a simplified pronunciation of Hathor (Egyptian goddess of love and fertility). Putting it all together, the phrase *ROTA TORA ORAT TORA ATOR* translates to "The wheel of tarot speaks the law of Hathor." Another way to express this would be "The cycle of tarot teaches the law of love." And if we want to bend it a step further, "The wheel of tarot teaches that love is the law." It wouldn't be a huge leap from here to see the Wheel of Fortune card as a big fat clue to the nature of tarot as a whole and the overarching wisdom that lies in the cards.

WINGS: Though the wings in this card are primarily part of the tetramorph symbol, there is another layer to this symbol that applies to this card. The Roman goddess Fortuna was often depicted with wings. She is the goddess of luck, chance, and fate. The firstborn child of Jupiter, she was an extremely popular goddess in ancient times. During the Middle Ages (*long* before the RWS tarot) she was often depicted in paintings with . . . you guessed it . . . a rotating wheel of fortune. She was originally a farming goddess associated with prosperity and abundance, and her symbols included a cornucopia. While she most definitely reinforces the concept of chance and the randomness of events in our lives, I believe her first incarnation brings up the idea of "you reap what you sow." In other words, is it all just up to fate and chance? Or are the events in our lives also at least partially a product of the effort we put in and what we choose to cultivate?

QUICK TAKES: Change is inevitable, luck is on your side; create your own luck. Indicates a life-changing chance meeting, an exciting new opportunity. What goes around comes around; check your attitude toward change; surrender control, embrace what comes next, winning games of chance. This too shall pass.

REVERSED: *mood swings, the start of a difficult time, unexpected change in circumstances.*

11. Justice

KEYWORDS: justice, truth, consequences, accountability, fairness, law, injustice, dishonesty, corruption, bias

ASSOCIATIONS

Astrological: Libra

Planetary: Venus

Elemental: air

Symbols

COLUMNS (PILLARS): structure, support, balance, strength, knowledge. The presence of two columns together typically represents a gateway to higher knowledge. Here, they represent the concept of being in the middle of two things, or in other words, impartiality. Their gray color also reinforces this. Equal parts black and white, gray indicates balance. In modern interior design practices, gray is considered the ultimate neutral—another great way to suggest the unbiased, neutral energy of Justice. In Qabalistic beliefs, the Tree of Life is described as having three pillars. Though there are only two shown in the Justice card, if we consider them to be the outer pillars "mercy" and "severity," they perfectly sum up the concept of Justice, representing a completely balanced middle point between forgiveness and the law of karma. (Or in other words, the idea of "you reap what you sow.")

CROWN: elevation, mastery, power, sovereignty, authority, intellect. The shape of a square symbolizes structure, balance, and logic. Its location on the crown emphasizes the ability to judge a situation with clarity. The square is also in the location of the third eye chakra, the energy center tied deeply to our intuitive abilities. This indicates that being fair and judicious requires both intellect and intuition.

CUBE: initiation, dominion, spiritual development, spiritual evolution. The Cube of Space is a three-dimensional structure that contains a dizzyingly complex system intended to represent varying degrees or grades of spiritual development. It also encompasses the 22 Major Arcana cards of tarot in its sugar cube-like dimensionality. This one is definitely deep dive-worthy and, in my opinion, amplifies authority over their domain.

SCALES: justice, balance, impartiality, possibility, truth, fairness, decisions, astrological sign of Libra. The ancient Egyptians believed that the heart recorded the deeds of a person's life, both good and bad. After a person died, the heart would be weighed on a scale against the feather of Ma'at, the Egyptian goddess of truth, justice, and balance. If the deceased had led a decent life, the heart would balance perfectly against the feather, and their journey to the afterlife would continue. If not, it would be game over. The afterlife was the be-all and end-all for the Egyptians, so the threat of potentially missing out colored their actions in their daily lives. In some ways, this can parallel the Christian concept of Hell and its use as a device to scare people into acting right. Both scenarios bring up symbolic themes around the importance of weighing our intentions and motives. The Egyptian heart-weighing ritual can also remind us not to stand in judgment of others, as we never truly know what's in another's heart. Furthermore, while the scales gently nudge us to strive for balance in our actions, it's also important to be mindful that we humans are inherently flawed creatures. We may be far from perfect, but we are always worthy.

SHOE: action, grounding, connection to the earth, humanity, consciousness, civility, protection. The white slipper represents the purity and truth that exist in true justice. As all shoes also indicate civility, here the slipper can also be seen as symbolic of the need for order and justice in a civilized society. Perhaps justice is one of the qualities that separates us from the animals.

SQUARE WITH CIRCLE: Squares typically represent the material world while circles represent the spiritual realm. This combined symbol (worn as a broach by the figure in the RWS tarot) indicates the sentiment "As above, so below"—or in other words, true justice stems from balance.

SWORD: element of air, intellect, power, discernment, decisiveness, truth, impartiality, purification, masculine principle, finality. The sword is a powerful symbol of justice. It represents the ability to cut through pretense and deception to discern the truth within a situation with perfect clarity.

QUICK TAKES: A fair outcome. Stand up for the truth, take the high road, find a solution in a situation that is fair to everyone involved, be willing to compromise. Indicates social activism, receiving what is owed, legal affairs, court cases, consulting a lawyer. Read contracts carefully before signing; trust that justice will prevail; balance your finances.

REVERSED: *refusal to take accountability, gossip, lies being told, racial profiling, jail sentence.*

12. The Hanged One

KEYWORDS: contemplation, waiting, surrender, perspective, limbo, transition, sacrifice, transformation, stagnation, delays, indecision, fear of letting go, victim mindset

ASSOCIATIONS

Astrological: none

Planetary: Neptune

Elemental: water

Symbols

FIRE: energy, warmth, desire, determination, transformation. There is no literal fire portrayed on the RWS tarot version of this card. But the hair of the character hanging upside down looks a bit like flames. Taking this a step further, in Hinduism and the practice of yoga, Kundalini energy is known as the "sacred fire" and thought to be an essential component in the process of spiritual awakening and attaining higher levels of consciousness.

MANNEQUIN'S POSE: waiting, limbo, unification, crossroads, perspective. *(Note: there are a total of four cards in* Tarot Disassembled *that show any hint at a human body whatsoever. I chose to use an artist's wooden mannequin when I felt the body told a story and needed to be included, but is also in line with leaving out all the baggage of human constructs.)* The pose of the Hanged One alludes to the numbers three and four: Their head and arms together form a trio and the triangular shapes made by their arms also indicate the number three. The legs form the shape of the number four. The number three denotes spirituality (such as in the Holy Trinity) whereas the number four represents the material or earthly realm (think of the four elements). Taking all the numerical symbology into account, the pose of the Hanged One represents the connection between the material and spiritual realms.

The crossed legs can also be seen to indicate being at a crossroads, which makes this even more important for aiding you in decision-making. The fact that this figure is upside down suggests that we sometimes need to see things from a different perspective to gain clarity on a situation.

Additionally, their position looks a little bit like the yoga pose *Vrikshasana* (known also as "tree pose"). Can you imagine the sheer number of things a tree witnesses and learns while staying in one spot for so many years? So maybe instead of the saying "make like a tree and leave," we should embrace the idea of "make like a tree and learn."

ROPE: confinement, control, will, joining, ascension. It's important to keep in mind that ropes not only bind and confine, but they can also be a tool for climbing or ascending higher—a perfect metaphor for seeking spiritual enlightenment.

STARBURST: light, hope, spiritual enlightenment. Originally shown as a halo behind the character's head in the RWS tarot, this burst of light adds an overwhelmingly positive message to what might otherwise seem like a bleak card. There is enlightenment to be found by being still and seeking a new perspective.

TREE: growth, potential, expansion, ascension, time. The tree found here is no ordinary tree. It is considered to be the World Tree—a motif found in multiple world cultures that connects the human world with the divine realm. My favorite take on this tree involves a story from Norse mythology. Yggdrasil is a sacred ash tree that houses the nine realms in its branches. It sits on top of the Well of Wyrd, a deep pool that holds the most powerful forces in the cosmos, including the magic of the runes. The powerful god Odin, known to be a relentless seeker of knowledge, "sacrifices himself to himself," and hangs himself from a branch of Yggdrasil, piercing himself with his spear. He hangs there for nine days and nights on the precipice of death until the runes finally accept his sacrifice and reveal their secrets to him. Could the Hanged One be Odin himself? I believe so, as this story so perfectly fits the energy of this card. If we see the tree as Yggdrasil, then the Hanged One takes on a much deeper meaning than simply waiting around. It speaks of willful surrender and sacrifice in order to obtain higher wisdom.

QUICK TAKES: Self-sacrifice for the greater good, spiritual growth, a time of metamorphosis. Look at a situation from a different angle, a fresh perspective, refrain from taking action at this time, wait it out. Indicates a renewal of mind and spirit, study of Buddhism.

REVERSED: *stuck in a rut, a narrow-minded point of view, high blood pressure.*

13. Death

KEYWORDS: change, endings, new beginnings, transformation, renewal, inevitability, fear of change, decay, lethargy, hopelessness

ASSOCIATIONS

Astrological: Scorpio

Planetary: Pluto

Elemental: water

Symbols

ARMOR: protection, shield, self-preservation, preparation, truth. In the RWS tarot, Death is portrayed as a skeletal figure dressed in armor upon a horse. If Death is the one that is protected, it's not a stretch to see the armor as symbolizing that death is unbeatable. With the Death card signaling endings and beginnings, you can be sure when it pops up that the ending that is coming or presently occurring is completely unavoidable. So why fight it? As armor also represents preparation, consider this card a heads-up that change is coming, and you'd best be prepared.

BOAT: journey, transition, refuge, death. Historically, world mythologies and cultural beliefs involving death are rich with boat imagery. The ancient Greeks believed that when you died, your soul would be transported to the afterlife via the river Styx by a ferryman named Charon. "Nothing in life is free" though, and apparently that also applies to the afterlife: loved ones were buried with a coin to pay Charon for transporting their souls. The Egyptians held a similar belief and carved ornate funerary boats out of wood to be entombed with the dead for use in their journey down the Nile to the afterlife. Other groups, such as the Dayak people of Borneo, had a version of a death ship as well. Beyond mere mythology, some cultures such as the Vikings conducted ship burials—the practice of burying the deceased in an actual boat or ship. The unifying symbolic meaning here is that of progressing from one state to another . . . a spiritual journey of sorts. I can't say it enough: the Death card is rarely about literal death but rather about endings and beginnings. Next time you look at that humble little boat symbol on the Death card, imagine all of the exciting new places this ending might take you.

CROWN: elevation, mastery, power, royalty, sovereignty, authority, intellect, divinity. You'll notice that the crown on the Death card is upside down. All of the power and grandiosity typically symbolized by a crown is no match for Death. In the words of Jim Morrison, "No one here gets out alive." That is to say, Death does not care if you are a king or a peasant. But as the Death card rarely indicates actual physical death and usually points to endings and beginnings, maybe the upside-down crown simply symbolizes a change in circumstances. Better yet, I like to think of it as symbolic of shedding what no longer serves us; getting rid of what weighs us down so that we can start fresh a little lighter. (That crown was too heavy anyway.)

FEATHER: freedom, hope, travel, ease of movement, change of direction, spiritual evolution, truth, judgment. In my opinion, the presence of the feather brings a lightness to a card that sometimes carries a heavy energy and evokes fear for some. The change that Death brings is nothing to be feared; embracing endings can be wonderfully freeing and can even stir up a sense of hope for the new beginning being ushered in. The less you resist this change, the easier you will move through it. The red color of Death's feather is symbolic of power. Death is a powerful force indeed, capable of bringing about big-time transformation.

In ancient Egyptian mythology, there is a story involving death and a feather. The goddess Ma'at was the goddess of truth, justice, balance, and order. After a person succumbed to death, they had to pass through the Hall of Judgement, where their heart would be weighed on a scale against Ma'at's feather of truth. If their heart balanced with Ma'at's feather, they could continue their journey to the afterlife. If not, their journey was over. The ancient Egyptians believed this was how order and balance were maintained in the universe. Similarly, the cycles of endings and beginnings we experience in our lives contribute to the order and balance of the universe.

FLAG: proclamation, attention, signal, authority, victory, herald. Flags typically indicate some type of big proclamation or announcement. In the case of the Death card, the black flag is announcing that something is most definitely coming to an end. Typically, this flag would appear with the white rose upon it, indicating that there is beauty in this ending, as well as the possibility for fresh growth (symbolic of a new beginning). (I have chosen to break both symbols out separately, keeping with the theme of this deck.) The black color of the flag also holds meaning: technically speaking, black is not an actual color itself but instead the absorption of all other colors of the spectrum. This is a beautiful metaphor for the universality of death and endings.

HORSE: status, momentum, movement, freedom, power, solar energy. Religious affiliations aside, most of us are familiar with the story of the four horsemen of the apocalypse found in the book of Revelation in the Christian Bible: "And I looked, and behold a pale horse: and his name that sat on him was Death." The white horse found on the Death card certainly can be attributed to this story. But just like everything in the tarot, there are deeper layers of meaning at play. Horses symbolize powerful movement and freedom—the change associated with the Death card can be representative of moving from one phase to another in our life (often bringing powerful transformation). There is also a beautiful sense of freedom inherent in surrendering to the inevitability of endings and beginnings heralded by the Death card. In Norse, Greek, and Roman mythologies there are stories of horses helping to pull the sun across the sky, linking them to the solar energy of this card.

ROSE: passion, vitality, enlightenment, secret wisdom, unfolding, illumination, transformation. Referred to as the "mystic rose," the white rose of the Death card represents purity and the innocence to be found in new beginnings. Much like the symbolism of the pentagram, the five petals represent the four elements plus the fifth unifying element of spirit. But beyond that, this rose is also a very specific rose, stylistically speaking. It is the white rose of York—the badge worn by the followers of the House of York in medieval England. Most famously, the white rose of York became counterpart to the red rose of the House of Lancaster; the two factions became embroiled in a fight for the crown known as the "War of the Roses." The conflict was eventually ended by King Henry VII of England, a Lancaster who unified the two houses by marrying Elizabeth of York. They symbolically united the white and red roses to create the Tudor rose and established the House of Tudor. What's all this Tudor history got to do with the Death card, you ask? Honestly, it's anyone's guess. We know the RWS tarot was the first to depict this very specific symbol. We know that Arthur E. Waite's mother was English. Beyond that, we know very little about what the true intentions of its inclusion were.

The War of the Roses transformed the history of the British monarchy. Perhaps we can see the rose as a nod to the transformation that is possible when the Death card appears. Alternatively, the association with the monarchy can be seen to reinforce the symbolism that the crown imparts—that Death (literal or figurative) is the great equalizer that affects kings and peasants alike.

One last wrinkle that comes to mind lies in the fact that the white rose of York signals the end of an era. The reign of any king is truly fleeting, just as the phases of our lives are. One king's reign ends, another begins. Therein lies Death's true meaning of the natural cycle of beginnings and endings.

SKULL: death, mortality, endings, passage of time, eternity. With its symbolic link to death, the skull can be a frightful symbol for some. But many cultures and periods in history have encouraged people to contemplate death. In medieval Europe, when plagues ravaged the population making death a daily occurrence, a new philosophy gained traction. *Memento mori*—which translates to "remember that you will die"—encouraged people to ponder death and remember their own mortality. While the Death card should not be regarded as a harbinger of imminent death, it's important to remember that none of us are getting out of here alive. Awareness that we are not given infinite time in this body tends to be just the kick in the pants we need to live life more fully.

SUN: life force, growth, cycles. The sun on the Death card is setting. Or is it rising? It's difficult to say for sure, but the meaning is the same either way. Are you familiar with the expression "just as sure as the sun will rise?" The cycles of the sun are unwavering in their constancy. So too are the cycles of beginnings and endings in our life. The sun is the perfect symbol to represent the beauty of rebirth that the Death card offers. I also find it perfectly fitting that the sun is so strongly associated with life force, as there can be no death without life.

WATER: emotions, life, movement, ebb and flow, purification, power, depth, intuition, subconscious. On one hand, the water shown on the Death card represents the natural flow in life from one stage to another, as well as the depth of emotions involved in the endings and beginnings heralded by Death. And just as water can cleanse and renew us, so too can we find renewal in the new beginnings we discover in life. Another facet of the water symbolism here is that it represents the river Styx, the river in Greek mythology believed to carry departed souls to the underworld. This too is a nod to the symbolism of flowing from one state to another. An oath sworn by a god on the river Styx was believed to be a binding contract. Breaking said oath could result in being paralyzed for one year and a day, or worse, having your Olympian god card revoked. This encourages us to approach new beginnings with honesty and truthfulness.

One last fun fact about the Styx: Thetis dipped her demigod baby Achilles in the Styx to make him invulnerable to harm. She held him by the ankle when doing so, leaving that the one spot on his body vulnerable. When the Death card pops up, consider whether your "Achilles' heel" is a resistance to change.

QUICK TAKES: A situation is coming to an end. Out with the old and in with the new; it's the end of an era, get rid of what no longer serves you, embrace change and personal transformation, resign from a job where you are not thriving, declutter your space, file for bankruptcy, divorce, quit a bad habit. It's time for a haircut; tomorrow is a new day.

REVERSED: *holding too tightly to something that is clearly over, fears around death and mortality.*

14. Temperance

KEYWORDS: balance, serenity, patience, moderation, peace, blending, imbalance, excess, discord,disharmony, overindulgence

ASSOCIATIONS

Astrological: Sagittarius

Planetary: Jupiter

Elemental: fire

Symbols

ANGEL: blessings, love, divinity, protection, messages. The specific angel depicted by the red wings on the Temperance card is the Archangel Gabriel. Each of the four primary archangels is associated with one of the four elements. Gabriel just so happens to be associated with the element of water, which ties beautifully to the other water symbolism on this card. Angels technically have no gender, but we humans still have a tendency to assign one to them. Interestingly, Gabriel is the only angel that is typically depicted as neither male nor female, making them a truly nonbinary figure. Temperance is all about perfect harmony and balance and, in this case, Gabriel can be seen to symbolize the perfect balancing of divine masculine and feminine energies within us.

CIRCLE WITH DOT: sun, gold, perfection, transmutation, attainment. The disc traditionally worn on the head of the angel in the Temperance card is the alchemical symbol for gold. One of the primary goals in alchemy is the transmutation of lesser metals such as lead into gold. For alchemists, gold represents the perfection of matter on any level, including the mind and spirit. Interestingly, the organ that gold corresponds to in alchemy is the heart. While modern chemistry has proven that turning lead into gold isn't technically possible, we can all still strive to achieve a "heart of gold." Perhaps love is the true key to transmutation.

CROWN: elevation, mastery, power, royalty, sovereignty, authority, intellect, divinity. In the RWS tarot, the imagery is subtle, but the sun is depicted here with an unusual configuration of rays, implying a crown. This can indicate a link to the crown chakra and opening ourselves up to the divine. Working in tandem with the path symbol, the crown can also be interpreted to mean choosing the higher path.

CUPS: element of water, emotions, intuition, receptivity, feminine principle. There is an implied alchemy happening with the pouring of the liquid between the two cups. It denotes the mixing, blending, and balancing of differing substances to make something new . . . something better. There's also a sense of striving for equal amounts between the cups . . . if you've ever shared a bottle of wine with friends, you've likely poured a little back and forth from each glass to try and fill the cups fairly. In that same way, the cups represent seeking equilibrium.

FEET: action, journey, travel, grounding, connection to the earth, humanity, consciousness, primal nature. One foot is shown dipping a toe in the water, while the other is shown standing on land. This depicts the union of the subconscious and the conscious. On a practical level, when we are feeling out of balance or overwhelmed in life, one of the easiest ways to center ourselves is the practice of grounding by walking barefoot on the earth.

IRIS: wisdom, messages, faith, purity. The Temperance card is associated with the Greek goddess Iris of the rainbow and messenger to the gods. While the iris itself holds meaning for this card, the greater meaning is in the presence of this rainbow goddess. Let's get our science on for a quick second: A rainbow is a multicolored arc made by light striking prisms, such as water droplets. It's also an optical illusion. The appearance of a rainbow depends on where you're standing and where the sun is in the sky. The sun is usually behind the person viewing the rainbow, meaning you are essentially standing between the sun and the rainbow. This is lovely metaphor for the beauty to be found in taking the middle path.

MOUNTAINS: aspiration, courage, retreat, perspective, ascension.

PATH: journey, life path, connectedness, boundaries, guidance. Though there is an overwhelming sense of peace and stillness with this card, the path indicates that there is still more work to be done on our journey to enlightenment.

ROCKS: element of earth, memory, gravity, permanence, rigidity, immovability, unwillingness to change. The rock suggests there is a balance to be found between going with the flow (water) and being fixed in our beliefs. The quality of being too rigid can imply an imbalance itself. The rock symbol also brings to mind Japanese rock gardens, whose purpose is to encourage meditation, calm, and a state of Zen (all energies of the Temperance card).

SQUARE WITH A TRIANGLE: The number three, represented by the triangle, denotes spirituality (such as in the Holy Trinity) whereas the number four represented by the square denotes the material or earthly realm (i.e., the four elements). Together they represent the divine balance between the material and spiritual realms.

STARBURST: light, hope, spiritual enlightenment. Originally shown as a halo behind the angel's head in the RWS tarot, this burst of light indicates the presence of the divine.

SUN: life force, joy, optimism, vitality, health, growth, cycles.

TETRAGRAMMATON: God, divine, being. The small white Hebrew letters near the top left corner of this card is the Tetragrammaton—the four-lettered name of God. In the RWS tarot, Pamela Colman Smith cleverly worked these characters into her illustration by detailing them into the folds of the angel's robes. It infuses this card with the presence of the divine, suggesting that we are aided in our efforts to seek balance between our spiritual and human natures.

WATER: emotions, life, abundance, movement, ebb and flow, purification, power, depth, intuition, subconscious. The peaceful, serene energy of Temperance is personified in the element of water. There's a reason why meditation/sleep CDs and apps are filled with the sounds of water . . . it evokes calm and tranquility the way no other element in nature can.

In addition to the sense of balance represented by the water being poured from one cup to the other, there is also a small body of water shown with one foot dipped in it (while the other is touching land). This symbolizes balancing our conscious and subconscious. The angel of this card, the Archangel Gabriel, just so happens to be the Archangel that oversees the element of water. In fact, it was by a water well that Gabriel delivered the message to the Virgin Mary of God's intention for her to be the mother of Jesus.

QUICK TAKES: Seek balance in imbalanced areas of your life; finding equilibrium strengthens your connection to the divine. Remain calm and rational in a tough situation. Relationship problems are resolved harmoniously; being patient with someone is an act of love. Indicates a blended family, a mixing of several things to create something new, artistic alchemy. Weigh your options carefully, connect with your spirit guides, balance your finances, go with the flow, commit to sobriety, a yoga practice, seek a mediator in a situation.

REVERSED: *imbalance in any area of life.*

15. The Devil

KEYWORDS: control, temptation, addiction, excess, materialism, negativity, deviance, shadow side, freedom, independence, release, personal power, detachment

ASSOCIATIONS

Astrological: Capricorn

Planetary: Saturn

Elemental: earth

Symbols

BAT: rebirth, illusion, echo, darkness, underworld. In some ways, bats are the ultimate creatures of darkness. They are nocturnal and able to see in situations we would consider pitch-black. While the Devil card may indicate that we are currently in a dark place, the bat symbol suggests that there may be something worth "seeing" or learning from this dark situation.

Bats are also amazing pollinators. They are responsible for pollinating over 700 different types of plants, many of which we use for food or medicine. How beautiful is that? If a creature of darkness can bring that much goodness to the world, perhaps the bat is here to teach us to see the beauty in our own shadow.

CHAINS: bondage, enslavement, limitation. The chains represent being enslaved by our bad habits, addictions, and baser natures. Being chained up means we are restricted or limited in our movement. You can think of this as your spirit being restricted from its natural state of expansion. When you see the chains, it's important to remember that the "Devil" is just a bit of fiction here. In reality, there is no demon or devil keeping you enslaved. In fact, you are your own jailer and have the power to break the chains that bind you whenever you choose.

FIRE: energy, warmth, lust, desire, determination, destruction, transformation. Fire can be destructive or renewing and transformative. The message of the Devil card is not that we should abstain altogether from giving in to desire, lust, or indulgence. (What fun would that be?) Rather, we should not allow those primal urges to burn out of control and consume us. Remember, in a forest a wildfire can ravage the land, but a controlled burn can be beneficial to new growth.

GRAPES: revelry, overindulgence, transformation, rebirth, redemption. Something I find fascinating: some sources suggest that the "Devil" character of this card is not Satan but rather Dionysus, god of grapes and wine—as well as ecstasy, pleasure, madness, and wild frenzy. In my mind this lightens some of the dark energy sometimes associated with this card. It is less about hell and damnation and more about facing the inner "demons" that we must keep in check. The debauchery inspired by Dionysus challenges us to determine where the line is for us. Surely, a little bit of occasional wild revelry can be good for the soul. But when we cross the line into excess and addictive behaviors, the same sweet grapes that made that pleasure-enhancing wine become toxic for us. Symbolically, the grape promises that redemption is possible if we take control of our negative behaviors and steer them back toward balance.

HAND GESTURE: If this symbol made you do a double take because it looks eerily similar to the "Vulcan salute" made famous by the beloved TV series *Star Trek*, don't worry . . . you're not crazy. It is indeed that very gesture. Leonard Nimoy, the actor who played Spock, was introduced to this gesture as a child at an Orthodox Jewish synagogue service where he saw it being used as a blessing, and later suggested using it in the now famous TV series. Nimoy gave an interview in 2013 explaining his understanding of the gesture's meaning. A *Washington Post* article by Abby Ohlheiser summarizes his explanation: "This is the shape of the letter shin." The Hebrew letter *Shin*, he noted, is the first letter in several Hebrew words, including *Shaddai* (a name for God), *shalom* (the word for hello, goodbye, and peace), and *shekhinah*, which is the divine feminine aspect of God that mothers, nurtures, and protects humanity.

Some think the hand gesture is meant to mock the ritual of the Hierophant. Others think it is a literal sign of the devil, with the two fingers on either side of the V representing the letters in the word itself. My personal interpretation of its usage here circles back to the Vulcan salute. The meanings inferred from the letter *Shin* bring a touch of divinity to this card, suggesting that God still blesses and loves us even at our worst. Also, with *shalom* meaning "peace," I believe this hand gesture prompts us to make peace with our shadow.

INVERTED PENTAGRAM: disharmony, misalignment, lust, evil, base energy, dark side of magic. The pentagram represents harmony and unification among the five elements (the fifth element being spirit). When the pentagram is inverted, it takes on the opposite meaning: disharmony and imbalance. In a pentagram, the top point of the star symbolizes spirit. In an inverted pentagram, that point is now facing downward, indicating that the primitive, material world has triumphed over spirit. The inverted pentagram also mimics the shape of a goat's head, tying this symbol back to Baphomet.

RAM: strength, power, determination, removal of obstacles, headstrong, ascension. In the traditional RWS tarot, the goat-headed figure is thought by many to be Baphomet, a neopagan horned god and a highly controversial, often misunderstood figure. Linked to the Knights Templar and famously illustrated by esoterist Éliphas Lévi, Baphomet is linked contemporarily to the Church of Satan (also highly misunderstood) and generically considered to represent all things evil. Baphomet has gotten a bad rap—the original intention of this androgynous figure may have been to symbolize the equilibrium of opposites:

human and animal, good and evil, male and female. Baphomet also represents the Freudian id of our psyche—the primitive, instinctual, immediate gratification part of our personality. All these meanings contribute beautifully to the overarching themes of the Devil.

Taking Baphomet out of the picture for just a sec, there are additional meanings brought to the table by the ram. The ram symbolizes removing obstacles from our path, suggesting that we have the power to break free from the challenges of our worst habits. Rams are also incredible climbers, indicating that we are capable of ascending or rising above our baser natures.

TORCH: enlightenment, hope, regeneration, guiding light, lust. While the torch encourages us to see the positive aspects of this card, it is also a phallic symbol—one that is on fire—signifying burning lust. The saying "carrying a torch for someone" comes to mind as representative of desire that has pervaded our thoughts to the point of being obsessive.

I also think of the dramatic shadows that are cast by torchlight. Perhaps the torch is symbolic of seeing and acknowledging our own shadow. The 20th-century psychologist Carl Jung is responsible for the concept of the "shadow self," and he summed up the beauty of it perfectly: "How can I be substantial if I don't cast a shadow? I must have a dark side also if I am to be whole."

The torch is also flipped upside down, indicating that someone might be pulling from base energies, rather than from divine light.

QUICK TAKES: Embrace your shadow side; owning your shadow leads to liberation. Confront your demons, recognize you are free to leave a bad situation. Indicates indulging in things or people that are not good for you: substance abuse, unhealthy sexual dynamics in a relationship, bad habits wreaking havoc, being bullied, a toxic person in your life. There is a need for spiritual cord-cutting; what you hate in others is mirrored in you.

REVERSED: *triumph over addiction, safely exploring BDSM, healing from a toxic relationship*

16. The Tower

KEYWORDS: chaos, disaster, disruption, destruction, revolution, rebuilding, unexpected, awakening, averting disaster, transformation, revelation

ASSOCIATIONS

Astrological: none

Planetary: Mars

Elemental: fire

Symbols

CLOUDS: element of air, constancy of change, turbulence, silver linings. The gray clouds of the Tower indicate that a storm is coming—or is already here. Batten down the hatches because it's gonna be a doozy. But just as clouds and the weather are ever shifting and changing, you can take heart that this storm will pass. The cloud symbol here also reminds us that even the most difficult events in our lives can have a silver lining. When the storm passes, assess the damage and look for yours.

CROWN: elevation, mastery, power, royalty, sovereignty, authority, intellect, divinity. Though crowns typically symbolize all things elevated and grandiose, the crown of the Tower card is shown in a topsy-turvy position indicating a fall from grace. In my opinion, one of the beauties of the Tower card is that it doesn't play favorites—disasters and calamity can happen to a powerful king just as easily as they can to a poor peasant. In that sense, we are all equal.

Also, since crowns are symbolically linked to the crown chakra, when this card pops up for you it's worth doing a little crown chakra check-in: Are you feeling disconnected, apathetic, cynical, uninspired, or exhausted? Those can all be signs of an unbalanced crown chakra. Activities that connect you to your higher self such as meditation, yoga, and positive affirmations can do wonders for an out-of-whack crown chakra. If you're having a true Tower moment in life though, chances are meditating and yoga are low on your list of priorities. But a little spiritual self-care certainly can't make the situation any worse, so what do you have to lose?

FIRE: energy, destruction, transformation. Fire, in some cases, can be tremendously beneficial for forests. It can clear the low-growing underbrush, opening up the forest floor to sunlight, nourishing the soil, and returning health to the ecosystem. Remember this when you view the fire symbols on the Tower card—the destructive energy of the Tower can also clear the way for better things.

There is a quote from Pablo Picasso that I feel captures not only the energy of this entire deck but is particularly fitting to sum up the dual nature of fire and the energy of the Tower as a whole: "Every act of creation is first an act of destruction."

LIGHTNING: sudden illumination, inspiration, destruction, force of nature, power. Lightning is symbolic of natural disasters and events that are completely out of our control, which is what the the Tower card represents. Lightning can also symbolize a sudden flash of inspiration and the type of eye-opening awakening that a Tower event can initiate in our lives.

Lightning bolts are also unequivocally associated with Zeus, the most powerful god in the Greek pantheon. But did you know that Zeus's lightning bolt was a gift? After rescuing his siblings from the stomach of their father (it's a whole crazy thing; look it up), Zeus then freed the Cyclopes (there were three of them), the brothers of Cronus, whom he had imprisoned. (Let's just say Cronus was kind of a dick.) As a reward for releasing them from Tartarus, the Cyclopes gave Zeus the gift of lightning. So when you see the lightning bolt, consider what gifts you might receive as a result of this Tower event.

The precise shape of the lightning strike is also intentional. It is made by playing an erratic game of connect the dots down the Tree of Life found in Qabalah. It represents the path of the descent of the divine into manifestation.

MOUNTAINS: courage, challenges, obstacles, perspective, ascension.

TOWER: ego, arrogance, material constructs, self-imposed limitations, possibility, defensiveness. The tower is symbolic of defense and protection. In medieval times, watchtowers were necessary to spot attackers from a mile away. Getting a heads-up that danger was on its way was a massive advantage in the game of survival. After all, mounting a defense is always much easier when you see it coming. Spiritually speaking, the tower may be encouraging you to be on the lookout for icky energy coming your way. Fortify your boundaries and energetic defenses accordingly.

***YOD* (י): divinity, spark of creation, building block, beginning, change.** The many yods depicted in this card add a touch of positivity to an otherwise unfavorable card to pull. As the Hebrew letter Yod is associated with the presence of the divine, the cataclysmic event at hand might actually be a divine blessing. There are also 22 yods, representing the 22 letters of the Hebrew alphabet. This implies that the Tower brings with it a sense of completion and totality.

QUICK TAKES: Big change is coming or is already here, so expect the unexpected, a painful or difficult life event, a big wake-up call, or spiritual revelation. Find awakening within the pain. Shocking information comes to light. Surrender control over what is out of your power; allow things to crumble so that you may rebuild. Indicates divorce, natural disasters, loss of a job, death of a loved one.

REVERSED: *being in denial about what is happening, clinging to old belief systems, resistance to big change, averting disaster.*

17. The Star

KEYWORDS: hope, inspiration, healing, optimism, faith, rejuvenation, peace, wish, manifestation, despair, disconnection, lack of faith

ASSOCIATIONS

Astrological: Aquarius

Planetary: Uranus

Elemental: air

Symbols

EIGHT-POINTED STAR: hope, guidance, balance. Eight-pointed stars show up in the symbology of a multitude of world cultures. In ancient Babylon, the eight-pointed star was an emblem of Ishtar. Ishtar, goddess of love and war, is associated with the planet Venus. From Earth, Venus appears to us as the largest, brightest star in the sky at dawn. Some have even speculated that the famed Star of Bethlehem that guided the wise men was, in fact, Venus, lending itself to the symbolism of guidance.

In addition to the one large star, seven smaller stars are shown, possibly representing the seven chakras, the seven metals of alchemy, or even the seven visible colors of the light spectrum. They also allude to the Greek mythological story of the seven sisters known as the Pleiades who were the seven daughters of Atlas—who himself was forced to hold up the sky for eternity. The hunter Orion fancied the sisters and pursued them relentlessly (translation: creepy stalker and predator) until Zeus stepped in and ended the ordeal by transforming them into stars. This reinforces the Star card's message of hope and renewal.

FLOWERS: hope, new growth, happiness, beauty, unfolding, renewal, love.

GREEN LANDSCAPE: abundance, growth.

IBIS: freedom, unrestricted possibility, ascension, enlightenment, lightness, messenger, wisdom, magic, writing. The ibis is associated with Thoth, the Egyptian god of writing, magic, wisdom, and the moon. These qualities pair beautifully with the magic and manifestation of the Star card. Thoth is credited with the invention of the written word, which reminds us that to harness the wish-making energy of the Star, you should write down what you wish to manifest into being.

JUGS: element of water, emotions, intuition, receptivity, feminine principle. The jugs hold a similar symbolism to the cups of the tarot and the pair of jugs hearkens back to the two cups seen in the Temperance card. The jug on the right is believed to represent our consciousness while the jug on the left is seen as representing our subconsciousness. I believe this may also correspond to certain holistic practices. Energetically speaking, the right side of the body is the masculine or giving side of the body, and the left side of the body is the feminine or receiving side.

TREE: growth, lushness, potential, sustainability, expansion, ascension, time.

WATER: emotions, life, abundance, purification, depth, intuition, subconscious. The two streams of water (one flowing back into water and the other nourishing the earth) together represent the cycle of life. They also represent the perfect balancing of opposing energies, the conscious and the subconscious, the physical and the spiritual, and the visible and the invisible. The five lines of the water symbolize the five senses we use to experience the physical world.

QUICK TAKES: Your wish is granted; dream big, have faith that everything will turn out wonderfully; good news is coming. Creative inspiration, being an inspiration to others, healing on all levels, healing professions, purification rituals, studying astrology. Take time for self-care, spend time in or near water to rejuvenate, take a bath.

REVERSED: *seek help or guidance when feeling hopeless, your faith is being tested.*

18. The Moon

KEYWORDS: illusion, intuition, subconscious, secrets, deception, dreams, uncertainty, duality, fear, clarity, secrets exposed, releasing fear

ASSOCIATIONS

Astrological: Pisces

Planetary: moon, Neptune

Elemental: water

Symbols

CRAWFISH: primal nature, ego, psyche, emergence, shedding, the past. The crawfish symbolizes our most primitive instincts. It represents a more primal nature than even the wolf on this card. The moon has the ability to bring out the deeply, animalistic side that lies within our human nature. (Need proof? Just ask anyone who works at an emergency room or police station how many more crazy incidents occur during a full moon.)

The crawfish is also a nocturnal creature that burrows and creates tunnels underground in watery areas at night. This makes it an apt symbol of the aspects of ourselves we attempt to keep buried that the moon can shed light upon.

Additionally, as the Moon can be a card of illusion—the crawfish's process of shedding its outer shell in order to grow can be seen to represent the need to shed illusions that limit us.

DOG: protection, communication, domestication, unconditional love. The dog and wolf work together like two sides of the same coin. I will discuss both symbols.

The dog represents our conscious, tamed mind which is fully within our control. I also believe the dog is indicative of the advanced intuition that is a key component of the Moon card. Dogs are highly intuitive animals; they are able to sense a human's moods and even sickness before they are themselves aware. Dogs also have a keen ability to sense whether someone is "good or bad" almost instantly upon meeting them. Their vision also differs from ours: humans can detect a broader color spectrum, but dogs have much better vision in the dark. How perfect is that for an association with the Moon card?

There is also a link between dogs and the moon via the Greek goddess Artemis (or Diana in the Roman pantheon). Artemis is the patron of the hunt, the wilderness, wild animals, all woodland creatures, and the moon. The god Pan gifted Artemis a pack of dogs to assist her when hunting. Artemis/Diana is also a moon goddess who is associated with both dogs and wolves.

MOON: intuition, cycles, emotions, divine feminine, the unconscious, shadow work, reflection, hidden information.

PATH: journey, life path, connectedness, boundaries, guidance. The path here represents the inner path we must journey on in our striving for self-discovery. This path is often fraught with the parts of ourselves we may not have faced before (symbolized by the fact that part of the moon is always in shadow and hidden from us): fears, suppressed traumas, and our shadow side, for example.

TOWERS: ego, arrogance, material constructs, self-imposed limitations, possibility, defensiveness, initiation. When towers appear in pairs in the tarot, they form a symbolic gateway. To pass between the gateway formed by the two towers, we must pass by human constructs and creations of the ego. Whether this gateway leads to enlightenment, higher knowledge or self-discovery, one thing is for sure: once you pass through this gate, you will be forever changed.

WATER: emotions, life, abundance, movement, ebb and flow, purification, power, depth, intuition, subconscious.

WOLF: primal nature, instinct, subconscious, ferocity. Wolves are, symbolically, the other side of the coin shared with the dog symbol. The wolf represents the wild, primal nature at the core of every human—the very source of our intuition. Both the dog and the wolf are necessary aspects of our selves, neither better than the other. Depending on what a particular situation calls for at the time, one might be more dominant than the other.

With over 200 million scent cells in their noses, wolves have an incredible sense of smell. This makes them symbolic of clairalience, the ability for a person to acquire psychic knowledge by means of smell. Have you ever suddenly caught a whiff of something with no explicable source? Just as some people can hear things others can't (clairaudience) and some can see things that others can't (clairvoyance), the wolf suggests this lesser-known psychic sense may be worth exploring in order to tap into the powerful intuition of the Moon card.

***YOD* (י): divinity, spark of creation, building block, beginning, change.** The Hebrew letter Yod is depicted 15 times in the same color as the moon itself, like little droplets of moonlight. This suggests that the secret knowledge the moon holds is divine in nature—the opportunities we are given for growth and change are gifts from God.

QUICK TAKES: Trust your intuition, develop psychic abilities. Things are not what they seem; the path ahead is unclear; you already know the answer. Indicates misunderstandings in a relationship, a false friend, being catfished. Honor your menstrual cycle, be in tune with your body's natural rhythms, pay attention to your dreams, nightmares, or insomnia, examine your phobias, face your fears head-on. Can indicate rampant anxiety or paranoia, hormonal imbalances, psychological conditions needing professional help, theater professions.

REVERSED: *the truth comes to light, releasing fear, clarity in a previously confusing situation, psychological conditions eased.*

19. The Sun

KEYWORDS: joy, happiness, abundance, success, optimism, vitality, confidence, inner child, fun, pessimism, overly enthusiastic, conceitedness, depression

ASSOCIATIONS

Astrological: none

Planetary: sun

Elemental: fire

Symbols

CHILD (represented by small shoes): Innocence, play, truth, boundless energy, generations, memories, inner child work.

FEATHER: element of air, freedom, hope, thought, lightheartedness, spiritual evolution, truth. Fans of the 1994 movie *Forrest Gump* will remember the lovely way a drifting feather opens and closes the movie. With all of the incredible events Forrest finds himself a part of, it's intriguing to ponder whether they were predestined or simply random. Above all, Forrest—who has the openness of a child—is a character who strives to be kind and good in even the most painful of situations. Whether our lives are a result of destiny or randomness, the feather paired with the positive energy of the Sun card teaches us that the moral of the story is to be our best selves no matter where the wind blows us.

FLAG: proclamation, attention, signal, authority, victory, herald. The flag on this card is a symbolic proclamation of victory over the darkness. The vibrant red color of the flag also links it to the root chakra, the driving force that imbues us with vitality and energy (much like the sun).

One of my favorite flag expressions is, "Let your freak flag fly." On a fundamental level, being authentically and unabashedly yourself takes immense courage, but the payout is huge. Like the radiant sun, the flag symbol invites you to take joy in shining your unique light for all the world to see.

HORSE: hard work, achievement, status, momentum, movement, freedom, power, solar energy. Thanks to Norse, Greek, and Roman mythologies, the horse is symbolically tied to the sun. Each has a story involving horses helping a god pull the sun across the sky.

Horses are also incredibly resilient animals. They sleep standing up and tolerate cold weather with ease. They also prefer sweet flavors and will reject anything sour or bitter. In my mind, this represents a willful rejection of bitterness and the prioritizing of more positive emotions, even in the face of tough times.

SUN: joy, optimism, vitality, health, growth, cycles, illumination, masculine principle, life force. There are exactly 21 rays of light radiating out from this particular sun. The summer solstice, the day with the longest amount of sunlight, often occurs on June 21st. The joy the Sun card ushers in is bound to be long-lasting. The number 21 also links this card to the World card. When you approach life with the luminous positivity of the Sun card, the world is yours to enjoy.

SUNFLOWER: confidence, energy, drama, nourishment, devotion, association with the sun, element of fire, association with Leo. All the keywords associated with the symbolism of the sunflower apply fully to the Sun card. But I particularly like the symbolic meaning of nourishment (derived from the yummy seeds this flower provides—for us and many grateful critters).

We are nourished on a deep, spiritual level by the emotions of joy and happiness.

WALL: boundaries, hurdles, protection, building up. There are a multitude of interpretations out there for what the wall of the Sun may symbolize. For the purpose of this book, I'll give you my personal take on it. The Sun is a happy, positive card indeed—possibly one of the most welcome cards in the deck. But the happiness indicated by the Sun takes effort to cultivate. That process can look much like constructing a wall . . . brick by brick, thought by thought . . . building up our self-esteem and view of the world with positivity and love. And once constructed, the wall acts as a boundary against all the ick that threatens to cloud our mood. (Please note, I am not trying to minimalize conditions like depression or suggesting we can eliminate sadness by simply "choosing happiness." I am talking bigger picture here, suggesting that on a mundane level we have a conscious choice over which thoughts we nurture and which we attempt to dismiss.)

QUICK TAKES: A divine gift, good news, cause to celebrate, success and good fortune. Let the good times roll, focus on what makes you happy, enjoy an easy time, boundless energy, unlimited joy, the power of positive thinking, practicing gratitude, being in the spotlight. Manifest anything you desire, share your light with others, take in awards and accolades, take a playful approach to a situation, lighten up and have some fun. Indicates pregnancy or adoption, inner child work, engagement, marriage, vacation to a sunny locale, working with your solar plexus chakra, athletic endurance.

REVERSED: *delayed success, feeling burned out, someone taking credit for your work, parenting stress, blocking your own success through negative thinking, being cocky or ungrateful about your success, time to grow up, feeling blue.*

20. Judgement

KEYWORDS: judgment, purpose, rebirth, awakening, absolution, passage, self-doubt, self-deprecation, error in judgment, false accusations, unwillingness to learn from the past

ASSOCIATIONS

Astrological: none

Planetary: Pluto

Elemental: fire

Symbols

ANGEL: blessings, love, divinity, protection, messages. This is a tricky one. While the angel represented here is most definitely an archangel, there are differing schools of thought on which one it is. The two contenders are Gabriel and Michael. I'm going to go out on a limb here and suggest that both apply. To start simply, each Archangel oversees one of the four elements. Gabriel's element is water and Michael's is fire. Both elements are featured here, suggesting both of their energies are present with this card.

Gabriel is the ultimate messenger angel. It was Gabriel who informed Mary that she would be the mother of the son of God. Gabriel also appears in the Bible delivering messages from God to Daniel and announcing the birth of John the Baptist. Most famously though, they are believed to be the angel that will blow the trumpet to announce Jesus's second coming. (The Bible never specifically mentions Gabriel as the trumpeter, but the association is there all the same.) I believe Archangel Gabriel is present in this card to share a message with us to wake up to our own divine nature. Gabriel's metaphorical trumpet sounds a call to action to step into our higher purpose.

Michael, on the other hand, is the ultimate protector angel. He is like the muscle of heaven—a warrior angel known for winning the battle against Satan. (Which also makes him a powerful angel to turn to when you could use some help removing negativity from your life.) But he is also known as the Angel of the Dead for his role in escorting deceased souls to heaven. No doubt, this role explains his possible link to this card. But just as the Death card is rarely about literal death, the Judgement card is less about the literal judgment day found in the Bible, and more about the possibility of big-time transformation and stepping into our higher purpose.

Angels are incredibly powerful entities, but above all they offer us loving guidance. In my opinion, their presence on this card imparts an overwhelmingly positive message accompanied by a reminder that there is angelic help available to us when we strive for a more meaningful life.

CLOUDS: thoughts, constancy of change, turbulence, silver linings, dreams, divinity.

COFFIN: death, transition, completion. The coffin can seem a scary symbol with its association to death. But it is not symbolic of literal death. Rather, it represents an opportunity to be reborn into a life where you are serving a higher calling or stepping into your true purpose. You'll notice a figure rising out of the coffin—this symbolizes heeding the call and "rising to the occasion" to embrace following a new path—one that honors the spark of divinity within you.

EQUAL-ARMED CROSS: balance, peace, oneness. Sometimes referred to as the Greek cross, the equal-armed cross represents the four elements. To the Ancestral Puebloans and in the ancient Middle East, it also represents the four directions (north, east, south, and west.) Both meanings imply a sense of completion and wholeness. In modern times, the red equal-armed cross is also an internationally

recognized medical symbol, used to identify nonpartisan medical services for victims of conflict regardless of national affiliation. In symbolic terms, redemption and healing are available to all, regardless of who they are or what they've done.

FIRE: energy, purification, transformation.

FLAG: proclamation, attention, signal, authority, victory, herald. The white flag of the Judgement card (in tandem with the equal-armed cross) proclaims that divine balance is being restored. The white color of the flag denotes innocence and purity. If the traditional Christian associations with judgment come up for you when you work with this card, you can take the white flag as a sign that even in view of all of our sins, at our spiritual core we are still pure.

MOUNTAINS: aspiration, courage, perspective, ascension.

TRUMPET: awakening, call to action, messages, announcement. The trumpet here alludes to the story of judgment day in the Bible: "And he will send his angels with a loud trumpet call, and they will gather his elect from the four winds, from one end of the heavens to the other." (Matthew 24:31) It heralds the second coming of Jesus and is therefore symbolic of a big-time announcement of something with transformative potential.

Yet even outside of the biblical influence of the trumpet, it is still a powerful symbol of awakening. Its cousin, the bugle, is famously used in the military to rouse personnel each morning. For anyone who's ever heard Reveille, you know it's not a gentle wake-up call. It will rip you out of a deep sleep faster than you can say "trumpet." The wake-up call of the Judgement card is similar in intensity.

Looking at the symbols of the trumpet and coffin together, I also can't help but think of a New Orleans jazz funeral (which for me, as a former inhabitant, has a personal nostalgia). The procession winds through the streets with the accompaniment of a brass band (heavy on the trumpet). Both grieving and festive in nature, the mourners typically dance wholeheartedly to the up-tempo music of the band. A symbol of rebirth, the New Orleans jazz funeral salutes a life well lived and the passage of a departed soul into a better world. Similarly, the potential for rebirth that is signified by the Judgement card is also cause for celebration.

WATER: emotions, life, abundance, movement, ebb and flow, purification, power, depth, intuition, subconscious. With the Judgement card, there is a theme of taking stock of your behaviors, choices, and actions in this life. Water reflects, and in this card it can be seen as symbolizing what is reflected back to you when you or someone else assess your actions. On the flip side of that coin, when we judge others too harshly, it is often because we see something in them that we don't like about ourselves—our judgment is reflected back at us, just like our own image in water.

QUICK TAKES: A rebirth is possible. Analyze your behavior; it's time to follow a new path; it's the dawning of a new era, a call to do what is morally right, time to take a good hard look at your actions. Strive to be a better person, live your life with meaning, follow a spiritual or religious calling. Indicates reincarnation, judging yourself too harshly.

REVERSED: *judging someone else too harshly, unethical behavior, ignoring your calling.*

21. The World

KEYWORDS: completion, wholeness, possibility, accomplishment, equality, connectedness, travel, lack of closure, incomplete, delays, unfinished business

ASSOCIATIONS

Astrological: none

Planetary: Saturn

Elemental: earth

Symbols

CLOUDS: element of air, constancy of change, silver linings, elevation, dreams, divinity.

DOUBLE-TIPPED WAND: divine inspiration, spiritual wisdom, will, conduit, harmony, perfect union, balance. The World card portrays two double-tipped wands . . . double the wands, double the power. A symbol that already signifies the concept of balance found in a pair only reinforces the idea of balancing dual concepts—conscious and subconscious as well as our inner world and outer world, working in perfect harmony. As the Fool also wields a wand of sorts (his staff), this symbol brings us full circle from the beginning of the journey presented by the Major Arcana.

LAUREL WREATH: victory, success, triumph, protection, wish fulfillment. When laurel is in the picture, themes of victory, triumph, and success aren't far behind. Both the Greek god Apollo and the Roman goddess Victoria are associated with the spicy sweet-smelling plant. With the themes of accomplishment and completion that accompany the World card, the laurel suggests that "the world is your oyster" and victory at the completion of any life goal is possible.

LEMNISCATE (INFINITY SYMBOL): infinity, eternity, perpetual motion, limitlessness, balance. The lemniscate of the World card perfectly reflects the nature of the Major Arcana itself. Many see the journey of the Fool through the Major Arcana as a perpetual loop rather than a straight line with a beginning and end. This reminds us that even though the World card is the final card of the Major Arcana, it does not represent a true ending but rather the completion of a phase or stage that ushers in a new beginning.

MANNEQUIN'S POSE: contentment, celebration, victory, future. The mannequin's pose here reflects the upside-down pose found on the Hanged One. With this figure now upright, the waiting game of the Hanged One is over and you have successfully completed this particular journey.

The World is a card of completion, but it also indicates moving forward to the next new phase. This is reinforced by the knee pointing to the right, moving toward the future. The figure also looks to be doing a little jig, suggesting there is reason to dance and celebrate getting to this point. Additionally, the legs make the shape of the number four, reiterating the harmonious balance between the four sets of energies brought in by the tetramorph.

The mannequin is also the color purple. In Qabalah, blue is the color of mercy, while red is the color of severity. When the two mix in equal parts, they create the perfect shade of purple. This color is new to the overall palette for *Tarot Disassembled*. I introduced it in a handful of cards in the second edition of the deck to impart the concept of balance between mercy and severity. The wholeness of the World card can only be achieved when things are divinely balanced.

TETRAMORPH (angel+eagle+lion+bull): A tetramorph is a composite of four symbols that act together to operate as a collective symbol. In this case, the angel, eagle, lion, and bull combine to create a tetramorph, previously seen in the Wheel of Fortune card. In Christian tradition, the four are associated with the four evangelists Matthew, Mark, Luke, and John. Another interpretation of this grouping associates each with an archangel and astrological sign. (Interestingly, these four signs are the fixed signs of the zodiac. The fixed signs are known for being go-getters who have the endurance to take ideas and bring them to completion.) This grouping simultaneously represents the four elements and corresponding four suits of the tarot. So, taking all that into consideration, we get: Lion—apostle Mark, Archangel Michael, Leo, element of fire, and suit of Wands; Eagle—apostle John, Archangel Gabriel, Scorpio, element of water, and suit of Cups; Bull—apostle Luke, Archangel Uriel, Taurus, element of earth, and suit of Pentacles; Angel (or human)—apostle Matthew, Archangel Raphael, element of air, and suit of Swords.

Together, they symbolize a harmonization between all of their collective energies. The World card indicates the completion of a cycle, but not an ending. A new beginning is being ushered in and the powerful tetramorph is here to guide you from one phase to the next.

YIN-YANG SYMBOL: duality, harmony, wholeness, balance. The yin-yang symbol represents ancient Chinese philosophical concepts: it represents the interconnectedness of the world and the natural harmony of opposites that cannot exist without their counterpart. There can be no positive without a negative, no light without shadow, and so forth. There is no yin-yang symbol in the RWS tarot, but the undulating shape of the cloth worn by the figure on the RWS World card looks a touch like the shapes within the yin-yang symbol. The meaning is also perfectly suited for this card, as it reflects the World's properties of balance, completion, and wholeness.

QUICK TAKES: Completion of a big project, achieving a lifelong dream, completing a major life lesson, successfully reaching a goal, seeking closure in a situation, a graduation, world travel, moving abroad. It is a reminder that we are all equal, all connected.

REVERSED: *unfinished business, a need to tie up loose ends.*

Minor Arcana

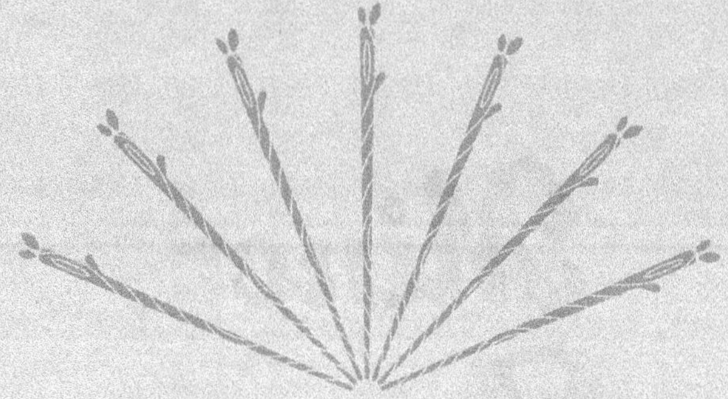

Wands

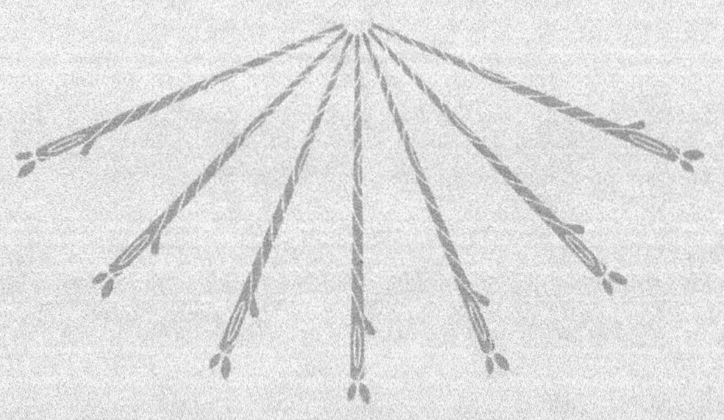

Ace of Wands

KEYWORDS: beginnings, creation, inspiration, passion, energy, new project, creative blocks, lethargy, uninspired

ASSOCIATIONS

Astrological: all fire signs—Aries, Leo, and Sagittarius

Planetary: none

Elemental: fire

Symbols

CASTLE: aspirations, attainment, future reward, wealth, power, comfort, fantasy, personal domain, protection. The castle in the Ace of Wands represents the potential expansion that is possible with the new ideas and inspiration that are brewing currently. It can also serve as a reminder to temper some of that fiery, creative energy with a stable and structured foundation.

CLOUDS: element of air, silver linings, elevation, dreams, divinity. All of the Aces in the tarot offer a gift or opportunity seemingly "out of the blue." The cloud symbolizes that this gift is divine in nature, heaven sent.

FIRE: energy, warmth, passion, determination, transformation.

HAND: giving, receiving. All of the Aces in the RWS tarot depict a disembodied hand emerging from the clouds. It represents that a gift of a divine nature is being offered when an Ace card appears. You'll notice that it is a right hand shown. Energetically, the right hand is considered to be the hand that gives while the left hand receives. A gift must be accepted willingly though, and an outstretched hand is what physically accepts a gift that is offered. So the hand also serves as a reminder that it is up to you to take advantage of the gifts and opportunities being offered to you at this time.

MOUNTAINS: aspiration, courage, perspective, ascension.

TREES: growth, lushness, potential, sustainability, expansion, ascension, time.

WAND: element of fire, spiritual realm, masculine principle, life force, energy, growth, vitality, willpower, conduit. This quote by Bryan Baeumler sums up the energy of the wand here beautifully: "Tools always seemed to have some sort of mystical power to me like a magic wand—in the right hands there's no limit to what they can do." Similarly, when the Ace of Wands is in play, there's no limit to the creative expansion and spiritual development you have access to right now, as long as you work your tools wisely.

WATER: emotions, life, abundance, movement, ebb and flow, purification, power, depth, intuition, subconscious.

YOD (י): divinity, spark of creation, building block, beginning, change. In Gematria, a numerological system in which Hebrew letters correspond to numbers, Yod is linked to the number 10, the number of change and beginnings and endings of cycles. The Aces in tarot are the first cards of each suit. Numerologically 10 breaks down to 1 (1 + 0 = 1). There are also exactly 10 yods on this card. All of this numerical energy hints at the expansive nature that accompanies the initial spark of inspiration or change the Ace of Wands brings. Think of it this way: when the yod is in play, your creative goals, hopes, and dreams have the potential to expand tenfold. It's like a divine gift that keeps on giving.

QUICK TAKES: Creative spark is at an all-time high; divine creative inspiration; a new idea being born; a resounding "yes!" to starting that new project, excitement and passion in the romance department. Physical energy and stamina abound.

REVERSED: *lack of inspiration, feeling uninspired and unmotivated, delays around starting a new project, romantic passions fizzling out, impotence.*

2 of Wands

KEYWORDS: planning, vision, control, discovery, progress, comfort zone, powerlessness, disruption, lack of planning

ASSOCIATIONS

Astrological: Aries

Planetary: Mars

Elemental: fire

Symbols

CASTLE: aspirations, attainment, future reward, wealth, nobility, power, comfort, fantasy, personal domain, protection.

CLOAK: mystery, protection, journey. As the 2 of Wands is a card of future planning, the journey may not yet be underway. But with the fiery red cloak in play, you can be sure the careful planning done today, infused with a sense of excitement and passion, will protect this new venture from failure.

GLOBE: possibility, exploration, travel, discovery, truth, expansion. Spoiler alert—the Earth is round! While this is likely not shocking new information to most of us, I was surprised to discover how long humans have been aware of this fact. The notion that the Earth is spherical has been around since at least the 5th century BCE, when some heavy-hitting Greek philosophers such as Aristotle began to tout the idea. Interestingly though, the ancients believed the globe included the earth *and* the heavens in its shape. One of the earliest representations of this concept is the 2nd-century sculpture *Farnese*

Atlas, which depicts the Greek Titan Atlas performing his task of carrying the weight of the heavens on his shoulders—only the "heavens" are lumped in with the Earth in one globular form. As Wands are the suit of the spiritual realm, the globe symbol imbues your ventures with a sense of divine purpose and heavenly guidance.

On a simpler note, the globe symbolizes that you hold the world in your hands at this time and the possibilities for expansion and discovery are limitless.

LILY: purity, virtue, innocence, knowledge. Once again, we see here a combination of lilies and roses together. The two work together in tandem to represent the need to balance the energies of the spiritual realm (lily) with the energies of the material realm (rose) to achieve your future goals. The lily also represents applying the knowledge of your life experiences thus far to your future planning.

MOUNTAINS: aspiration, courage, challenges, obstacles, retreat, perspective, solitude, ascension.

ROSE: passion, vitality, enlightenment, unfolding, transformation. It's no coincidence that the rose is emblematic of romantic love. The word is an anagram of Eros, the Greek god of love. As the myth goes, Chloris, the goddess of flowers, while out for a stroll in the woods, happened upon a lifeless nymph. Saddened by its death, she transformed it into a flower so beautiful that all the gods would consider it the Queen of Flowers. Aphrodite, the goddess of love, was so taken by its beauty that she named it "rose" in honor of her son, Eros. As twos in the tarot are suggestive of potential partnership, the presence of the rose on this card suggests that future romance may be on the horizon.

WALL: boundaries, hurdles, limitations, protection, building up. The 2 of Wands is a card of planning, and the wall signifies that careful planning will ensure that any obstacles you encounter on this next leg of your journey will be easily overcome. Alternately, the wall can indicate that you are reluctant to leave your comfort zone and move forward with your plans (particularly if this card is reversed).

WANDS: element of fire, spiritual realm, masculine principle, life force, energy, growth, vitality, willpower, conduit.

WATER: emotions, life, abundance, movement, ebb and flow, purification, power, depth, intuition, subconscious.

QUICK TAKES: Make a clear action plan, take control of your situation, take big risks. Indicates long-term planning, expanding your horizons, creating a road map to success. Multiple options for success are available to you. World travel.

REVERSEDS: *a change in plans, delays in travel, failure to make a solid action plan, success goes to your head, finding yourself at a crossroads, unwillingness to step out of your comfort zone, stop playing small.*

3 of Wands

KEYWORDS: expansion, adventure, foresight, opportunity, travel, confidence, setbacks, limitations, obstacles

ASSOCIATIONS

Astrological: Aries

Planetary: sun

Elemental: fire

Symbols

BOAT: navigation, journey, transition, expansion. A boat can symbolize expanding our horizons, an energy that is perfectly captured in the 3 of Wands. Three is a number associated with creativity, and the three boats represent that our creativity can take us places, leading to expansion on all levels.

CHECKERED SASH: opposing forces, contrasting ideas, duality, extremes, balance, danger. The presence of three wands may indicate a venture in which you are collaborating with others. In this case, the checkered sash can indicate the need to find balance amid opposing opinions within this group. You may not all see eye to eye on how things should be done, but you should strive to find middle ground for the benefit of all. If it's a solo journey you're on—perhaps one of a spiritual nature—the light and dark squares symbolize your own contrasting light and shadow sides. One of the primary energies of the 3 of Wands is expansion. Expansion rarely occurs in our life when we deny our own shadow. So give that shadow of yours a little love and maybe even a cookie, and you'll be amazed at the expansion that starts to occur in your life.

In nature, the pairing of yellow and black together often means "danger!" Bees, wasps, and certain species of poisonous frogs and venomous snakes don these colors as a warning that it's best not to mess with them. The type of big-time expansion that the 3 of Wands brings rarely comes without a bit of risk. But in the words of Niccolo Machiavelli: "Never was anything great achieved without danger." Know the risks, sure. But do it anyway.

CLIFF: jumping-off point, threshold, faith, unknown, vantage. Standing at the edge of a cliff may be a bit scary, but man, the views are phenomenal! This card is all about expansion, and the cliff symbolizes that a willingness to be bold and brave is often rewarded with an understanding of the big picture. From this vantage point, it is clear that the options available to us are limited only by the limitations of our vision. Adventure is calling: take that leap!

CLOAK: mystery, protection, journey. The red color of the cloak indicates the need to bring your passion along with you on this journey.

GREEN LANDSCAPE: fertility, abundance, growth. The green earth complements the energy of fire with a stabilizing, grounding influence.

MOUNTAINS: aspiration, courage, challenges, obstacles, ascension.

WANDS: element of fire, spiritual realm, masculine principle, life force, energy, growth, vitality, willpower, conduit.

WATER: emotions, life, abundance, movement, ebb and flow, purification, power, depth, intuition, subconscious.

QUICK TAKES: Big-time expansion, hard work paying off, moving forward with plans. Opportunities abound, broadening your horizons through learning or overseas travel. Spread your wings, take things to the next level.

REVERSED: *lack of growth, obstacles to your plans, frustrating delays and setbacks, time to go back to the drawing board.*

4 of Wands

KEYWORDS: celebration, bliss, harmony, foundations, home, transition, personal celebration, instability

ASSOCIATIONS

Astrological: Aries

Planetary: Venus

Elemental: fire

BOW: adornment, gifts, surprises, opening, love, innocence, perfection. Bows are synonymous with gifts, and the 4 of Wands most definitely comes bearing gifts. Having a cause to celebrate is a gift in and of itself, but this card may also indicate bigger-picture gifts that are life-changing. I can't list all the possibilities here . . . Untying a bow on a gift leads to unexpected surprises. Who's to say what surprises this card has in store for you? The saying "put a bow on it" means to put the final touch on something to make it perfect. When this card pops up, there is a sense of perfection about this moment in time. Allow yourself to enjoy it.

BRIDGE: overcoming obstacles, connections, passage, new direction, stability. As the 4 of Wands is a card of big celebrations, the bridge serves to represent crossing over into an exciting new phase of life.

CASTLE: aspirations, comfort, future reward, wealth, personal domain, attainment, refuge, protection. Medieval castles housed an average of 200 people within their walls. In this card of celebration, the castle also symbolizes the sense of togetherness and community we experience when we celebrate our greatest joys with others.

FLOWERS: growth, happiness, hope, love, new growth, unfolding, renewal, cycles. Some of the flowers here are gathered into a bouquet. We all know what that means. This card can sometimes herald a wedding, and the bouquet really drives this message home.

GRAPES: abundance, prosperity, revelry, celebration, blessings, sweetness of life, overindulgence. As the 4 of Wands is a card of celebration, the symbolism of the grapes here wouldn't be complete without a nod to Dionysus, Greek god of grapes and wine. (Or Bacchus, his Roman counterpart.) The original party boy, he was also considered the god of ecstasy, pleasure, madness, and wild frenzy, enhancing the humble grape's association with revelry and celebration.

In addition to all that crazy fun, here's a little something new that I discovered about Dionysus. Dionysus is the one who gave King Midas the ability to turn everything he touched into gold. He was so excited about this new ability that he ordered his servants to prepare a feast to celebrate. But he could no longer enjoy the food or drink because his touch turned it all to gold. Sadly, he also turned his own daughter into gold. So in a roundabout way, the grapes also serve as a gentle reminder to those planning a big celebration not to obsess over the material details too much. It's not about how grand the decorations are or how expensive the food is, it's about the joyful time spent with family and friends. (Oh, and in case you're wondering, that story has a happy ending. King Midas learned from the error of his ways and Dionysus graciously lifted the curse and restored his daughter.)

ROSE: love, passion, vitality, unfolding, magic, illumination. In Eastern traditions, the rose is linked to the heart chakra, the energetic center of love for ourselves and others, as well as empathy, compassion, and forgiveness. The love energy of the heart chakra is deeper than mere romantic love. It encompasses the unconditional love we feel for those we are most connected to, as well as the love we give to ourselves. The celebrations and foundations represented by the 4 of Wands are undoubtedly rooted in love.

WANDS: element of fire, spiritual realm, masculine principle, life force, energy, growth, vitality, willpower, conduit.

QUICK TAKES: There's reason to rejoice—a major milestone, a time of jubilant celebration—so take a moment to reflect on how far you've come; share the joy of your achievements with friends or family. Indicates harmony on all fronts, long-term partner potential, a wedding, returning home, harmonious family, a family reunion, a new home or home renovations, work/life balance.

REVERSED: *privately celebrating a personal milestone, surprise party, moving to a new home or leaving home for the first time, problems on the home front, party planning complications.*

5 of Wands

KEYWORDS: competition, conflict, disagreements, strife, tension, assertiveness, peace, truce, agreements, escalation

ASSOCIATIONS

Astrological: Leo

Planetary: Saturn

Elemental: fire

Symbols

GRAPES: overindulgence, revelry, sweetness of life, redemption. Though the 5 of Wands can indicate conflict and strife, I believe the energy here is more in line with a frat party that just got a little out of control. That would be perfectly in tune with the chaotic energy that Dionysus (god of grapes and wine) brings to a party: pleasure and celebration turning to wild frenzy with a touch of madness. The grapes also symbolically promise the members of this conflict that redemption is possible. (Likely after everyone has chilled out and apologized.) One of Aesop's fables, "The Fox and the Grapes," brings another meaning of grapes. The story goes that a fox was attempting to eat grapes from a vine but could not reach them. Too prideful to admit defeat, he instead claimed he didn't really want them anyway. This is thought to be where we get the expression "sour grapes." Someone in the group reflected in the 5 of Wands may be sour over something, leading to an all-out row.

LANDSCAPE: While a green landscape symbolizes growth and abundance, this yellowish patch of land appears parched and unlikely to grow anything. Just as the fiery warmth of the sun can bake the earth in the absence of water, the fiery energy we bring to a situation can halt growth when we allow it to blaze too hot in the form of anger and impulsiveness.

POLKA-DOT TUNIC: I adore this quirky symbol. In the RWS tarot, the figures battling on this card wear a variety of colors and clothing. But one individual has come to this fight wearing a polka-dotted tunic. If there was ever an indication that this fight is a spirited, good-natured competition, this is it. Seriously, who wears polka dots to a real battle?

SHOES AND BOOTS: action, journey, grounding, connection to the earth, humanity, consciousness, civility. There are a total of five pairs of shoes and boots shown on this card, representative of the five figures shown battling on the RWS tarot. The variety of colors indicates that everyone is bringing a different energy to this fight, and as this "fight" may actually be verbal in nature—the colors can be seen to symbolize the variety of opinions and viewpoints brought to the table in a spirited debate. The boots and shoes can also be considered a literal symbol of "standing your ground" in a conflict.

This card can also indicate a need to choose your battles wisely. Nancy Sinatra's lyrics, "these boots are made for walking," spring to mind. Perhaps the shoes and boots are suggesting that sometimes it's better to simply walk away from a fight rather than waste any more precious energy on it.

WANDS: element of fire, spiritual realm, masculine principle, life force, energy, growth, vitality, willpower, conduit. The wands here appear in a jumbled mess, indicating the chaotic energy of the current conflict. As Wands are the suit of fiery creativity, this jumble of wands can also represent a multitude of creative ideas vying to come to the forefront. There's no lack of creative spark here, but there is internal conflict over which idea to give your focus and energy to.

QUICK TAKES: Healthy competition, a spirited debate, everyone shouting to be heard, ongoing disagreements, standing your ground, power struggles in the workplace or within a team, too many type A personalities in the mix, picking a fight, internal conflict over a situation, the need for physical activity as an outlet for anger or irritation, hormonal imbalances.

REVERSED: *an end to the fighting, finding middle ground, coming to an agreement, taking things too far, it's all fun and games until someone gets hurt, feeling defeated, being bested, choose your battles wisely.*

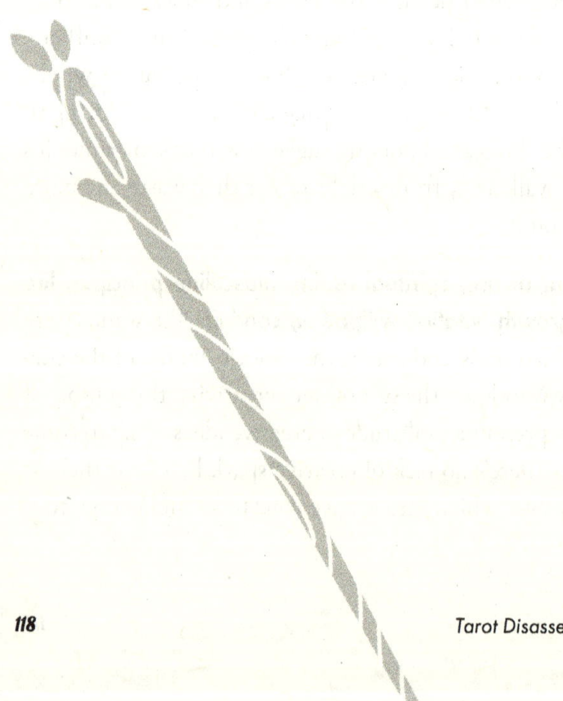

6 of Wands

KEYWORDS: victory, success, winning, recognition, confidence, awards, self-doubt, fall from grace, losing

ASSOCIATIONS

Astrological: Leo

Planetary: Jupiter

Elemental: fire

Symbols

BOW: adornment, gifts, surprises, opening, love, innocence, perfection.

CIRCLE WITH A LINE: In the RWS tarot, the wand held by the victor is adorned with a circular laurel wreath. Together, the wand and wreath form the shape of a circle with a line through the middle. Symbolically, this may be one of two things. The first is the alchemical symbol for salt. In the practice of alchemy, salt is one of three substances, along with mercury and sulfur, comprising the "three primes" or *tria prima.* Salt is impure when first collected, but can be purified through the process of dissolving, symbolizing a purity of mind and spirit that has led to this achievement. Salt is also present in our blood, sweat, and tears, suggesting that you have arrived at this point of triumph through a great deal of hard work and sacrifice.

The other possibility is that this symbol is the Greek letter *theta.* Theta was derived from the Phoenician letter *teth*, which meant "wheel." This ties back to the energy of the Chariot card, another card that indicates victory. The movement indicated by this "wheel" brings up questions like, "Where will this victory take you?" and "How far will it propel you?"

CLOAK: protection, journey, regalia. Success at last! The vibrant red cloak is befitting of the pomp and circumstance associated with this well-earned victory.

HORSE: hard work, achievement, status, momentum, fortitude, movement, freedom, power, solar energy. The horse is dressed for a regal celebration in a green caparison. The color green indicates abundance, growth, prosperity, and healing—all things that can stem from a great achievement or victory.

Chincoteague and Assateague Islands, located just off the coast of Virginia, are home to a group of wild horses that have adapted to their surroundings by developing the ability to drink small quantities of salt water when fresh water is unavailable, thus building a tolerance to a potentially dangerous substance. It's an unfortunate truth that the higher the level of success you attain, the more the haters come out of the woodwork seeking to tear you down. The horse symbol here may be nudging you to be tolerant and remain unaffected by the salty shenanigans of those jealous of your victories.

LAUREL WREATH: victory, success, triumph, higher learning, wish fulfillment. Laurel reinforces the energy of victory inherent in this card. Laurel wreaths were sported by the earliest winners of the Olympic games, symbolic of their great achievement. The laurel also hearkens back to the Chariot card, another card synonymous with victory. Laurel is also one of the emblems of the Greek god Apollo. Apollo was (among a litany of other things) the god of the sun. Though there is no sun depicted here, the association with Apollo makes the laurel a symbol of "having your day in the sun."

Another relevant association with Apollo is the Terrace of the Lions. On the island of Delos in Greece there once existed a series of lion sculptures dedicated to Apollo erected by the people of Naxos around 600 BCE. In a roundabout way, the laurel wreath reinforces this card's association with the astrological sign of Leo.

WANDS: element of fire, spiritual realm, masculine principle, life force, energy, growth, vitality, willpower, conduit.

QUICK TAKES: Victory is yours; you receive recognition for your achievements. Awards and accolades, embracing self-confidence, being in the spotlight, coming out of challenges triumphant, winning in legal battles, winning any type of competition, a big promotion.

REVERSED: *letting self-doubt get in the way of success, not believing you have what it takes to win, a falling out of favor at work or in the public eye, losing a competition you thought you had in the bag.*

7 of Wands

KEYWORDS: challenge, tenacity, conviction, defense, opposition, resolution, giving up, overwhelm, exhaustion

ASSOCIATIONS

Astrological: Leo

Planetary: Mars

Elemental: fire

Symbols

CLIFF: danger, risks, challenges, faith, vantage. The cliff has a slightly different energy here than when it shows up on previous cards. In this case, the individual is standing their ground in a fight, possibly backed up to the edge of a cliff. If they give in to exhaustion or give up, one good blow may send them toppling over. Metaphorically speaking, they have taken the highest position in the battle, reinforcing the theme that tenacity and determination are qualities that elevate us. Even in the face of adversity (like the potential harrowing drop off that cliff), they are sure to emerge triumphant, as long as they stand their ground.

GRASS: elements of earth and water combined, growth, expansion, community, interconnectedness. The fact that grass is growing so strong and lush on such a high, rocky cliff is a feat in itself. If grass can thrive when things get rocky, so can you. Grass can also be symbolic of community since it never grows alone. This can represent the need to call for backup in this conflict.

SHOES: action, journey, grounding, connection to the earth, humanity, consciousness, civility, protection. The person engaged in this battle has come to the fight wearing two different shoes. The situation at hand may have sprung up seemingly out of nowhere, giving you little time to prepare. No matter; you can still bring your full energy to the table even at a moment's notice. Wands are associated with the element of fire, which needs very little time to build to a powerful blaze.

WANDS: element of fire, spiritual realm, masculine principle, life force, energy, growth, vitality, willpower, conduit.

WATER: emotions, life, abundance, movement, ebb and flow, purification, power, depth, intuition, subconscious. In the RWS tarot, there is only a very small hint at water present at the top of the cliff where the character makes their stand. It seems only logical that this water would cascade off the edge of the cliff resulting in a waterfall. The downward motion of a waterfall represents a powerful force being unleashed; therefore, the water here can be seen to represent a need to summon all your energy and "rain down hell" upon your aggressor. As water almost always carries the symbolism of the emotional realm, it's fair to assume the water indicates that this fight may be emotional rather than physical in nature. Either way, prepare to fight the good fight.

As the energy of this card indicates a fight of sorts, I also adore the relevancy of this water-themed quote by martial artist Bruce Lee: "Be like water making its way through cracks. Do not be assertive, but adjust to the object, and you shall find a way around or through it."

QUICK TAKES: Defend your seat of power, stand up for what you believe in, stand up to bullies, others trying to knock you off your pedestal. You may be the target of jealousy; reinforce your boundaries, hold your ground against opposers, protect your investments.

REVERSED: *finding common ground with your enemy, exhaustion from battle, rebuild your self-confidence, throwing in the towel, fighting a losing battle, retreat and regroup.*

8 of Wands

KEYWORDS: speed, movement, rapid change, action, travel by air, frustration, waiting, procrastination, patience, slow pace

ASSOCIATIONS

Astrological: Sagittarius

Planetary: Mercury

Elemental: fire

Symbols

ARROWS: future, trajectory, targeting. The arrows reinforce the forward movement and progress indicated by this card. As they are pointing to the right, they represent looking toward the future. The swift changes and action brought on by this card will undoubtedly shape your future. The act of shooting an arrow also symbolizes clear purpose and intent—your eye is on your target and your aim is true.

GREEN LANDSCAPE: fertility, abundance, growth.

HOUSE: home, comfort, security, family. The house represents that your aims and goals may be lofty but are built on a solid foundation. You are safe to soar.

WANDS: element of fire, spiritual realm, masculine principle, life force, energy, growth, vitality, willpower, conduit. The eight wands here are shown flying through the air, almost like javelins thrown with the aim to achieve as much distance as possible. This is the energy of being propelled and swiftly changing location. When the 8 of Wands pops up, prepare for rapid change in your life.

Additionally, some have proposed that the wands allude to Jacob's ladder in the Bible. In Genesis 28:10-21, Jacob has a dream of a ladder stretching up to heaven, symbolizing a divine connection between the earthly and spiritual realms. As Wands are the suit of the spiritual realm, I think this is a lovely symbol for the possible spiritual growth we can experience by progressing on our path.

WATER: abundance, movement, ebb and flow, power. The energy of this card is all about forward movement and progress, so the stream shown here is symbolic of that same free-flowing, rapid-moving energy.

QUICK TAKES: Rapid progress and forward movement; full steam ahead; rapid life changes for the better; get it while it's hot; quick completion of a project; seize the day; travel via airplane.

REVERSED: *significant delays, putting off tasks, be patient with the process, a period of waiting, slow progress is still progress, getting your ducks in a row in order to move forward.*

9 of Wands

KEYWORDS: perseverance, resilience, determination, boundaries, struggle, hope, exhaustion, defensiveness, stubbornness, distrust, paranoia

ASSOCIATIONS

Astrological: Sagittarius

Planetary: moon

Elemental: fire

Symbols

BANDAGE: wound, injury, emotional pain, struggle, healing. The bandage indicates feeling beat-up by present circumstances or struggles, but it also is a sign that healing is possible.

The ancient Greeks and Romans used spiderwebs to keep wounds dry and prevent infection, just as we use modern-day bandages. (So, if Spider-Man ever gets tired of being a friendly, neighborhood Spider-Man, I guess he would make a ER doctor.) If you're feeling metaphorically beat-up, as the 9 of Wands suggests, let spiderweb bandages inspire you to find a creative solution to end the struggle at hand.

BOOTS: action, journey, travel, grounding, connection to the earth, humanity, consciousness, civility, protection. The expression "stand your ground" is perfectly fitting for the boots on this card. You may feel beat-up from your challenges but stay standing. It won't be much longer until you can take a load off and rest. The green color of the boots also symbolizes abundance, growth and healing—all of which will come as a result of your unwavering resilience.

On the flip side (particularly when this card is reversed), there's a fine line between knowing when to dig deep and keep fighting and when to call it quits for the sake of your best interest. This card can indicate a stubborn refusal to give up the fight, even when it's clear you're in too deep. There is a famous pair of green boots on Mount Everest that tells just such a sad tale. Over 200 deaths have occurred from failed attempts to climb this mountain, and tragically, many of the frozen bodies remain there. The most famous of these was the discovered body of a man wearing bright green boots. He serves as a grave reminder to know and honor your limits.

MOUNTAIN: aspiration, courage, challenges, obstacles, retreat, perspective, solitude, ascension. The 9 of Wands suggests the challenges leading up to this moment have likely been brutally difficult. But it's also likely that you are almost at the peak and the worst of this challenge is over. The feelings of satisfaction and pride that come from a hard-earned win will make the tribulations worth it. An anonymous quote sums this up nicely: "The best view comes after the hardest climb."

STAGE: fantasy, illusion, overdramatization, perspective, story. In my opinion, the stage in the 9 of Wands is deeply linked to the stories we tell ourselves. The 9 of Wands indicates extreme exhaustion from an ongoing battle. It would be so tempting to give up and admit defeat right now—at least then you could rest. To muster that last ounce of hope and determination may require telling yourself a tall tale. Tell yourself, "I'm not tired." (Even though you are beyond exhausted.) Tell yourself, "I've got this." (Even though that may feel far from the truth.) You can even embrace your inner Captain America and tell yourself, "I can do this all day." Sometimes a little bit of fantasy is all you need to rekindle your determination.

WANDS: element of fire, spiritual realm, masculine principle, life force, energy, growth, vitality, willpower, conduit.

QUICK TAKES: Keep pushing—you're almost there. Stand tall in the face of adversity, confront your challenges head-on. Indicates a test of faith, overcoming many trials and tribulations, rocky or draining relationships. Safeguard yourself from the negativity and drama of others, heal past wounds (emotional or physical) in order to move on. Migraines and health problems concerning the head, winning the battle against ongoing health problems.

REVERSED: *failing to set healthy boundaries, past betrayal leads to distrust of others, unnecessary paranoia, being overly defensive in a situation, let down your guard, stubbornly refusing to back down, pushing yourself to the point of extreme exhaustion.*

10 of Wands

KEYWORDS: accomplishment, success, responsibility, burden, burnout, breakdown

ASSOCIATIONS

Astrological: Sagittarius

Planetary: Saturn

Elemental: fire

PLOUGHED FIELD: preparation, new growth, fertile land, new creative ideas. The ploughed field here embodies the sentiment "you reap what you sow." You will get out of this experience what you put in. If you give it your all and see it through to the end, then you will be rewarded with growth and abundance from your efforts. If not, then the resulting crop will reflect that. As 10s in the tarot signify the completion of a cycle, the ploughed field is also a promise of the fresh new beginning that is just around the corner after finishing this phase.

TOWN: expansion, achievement, civilization, possibility, rest, time. The town symbolizes that the strong work ethic indicated by this card leads to growth and expansion over time. But the heavy load of the 10 wands also suggests that this town can be a much-needed place of rest. The question is, will you allow yourself to put down that load you're carrying and rest? Doing so may help you avoid burnout.

TREES: growth, lushness, potential, sustainability, expansion, ascension, time.

WANDS: element of fire, spiritual realm, masculine principle, life force, energy, growth, vitality, willpower, conduit. The wands here are gathered in a bundle, symbolizing a heavy load or burden that you are carrying at this time. As tens in the tarot signify completion, the end is in sight and you can put down that heavy load soon.

QUICK TAKES: One last push to the finish line; the end is in sight; a strong work ethic; taking on a heavier workload; success brings its own set of problems; feeling weighed down by your responsibilities; overextending yourself; a need to delegate responsibilities and share the load; a need to rest and recharge.

REVERSED: *working to the point of burnout, know your limits, time to shed some of your burdens.*

Page of Wands

KEYWORDS: inspiration, vitality, exploration, potential, ideas, creativity, education, good news, unimaginative, lazy, rebellious, bad news

ASSOCIATIONS

Astrological: none

Planetary: none

Elemental: fire, earth

Symbols

BOOT: action, journey, travel, grounding, connection to the earth, humanity, consciousness, civility, protection.

FEATHER: freedom, hope, travel, ease of movement, change of direction, thought, lightheartedness, spiritual evolution. In addition to representing the lighthearted spirit of the Page of Wands, the feather also symbolizes the spiritual evolution that is present with this card. After all, the Page will eventually evolve to become the Knight if they successfully progress on their path.

FIRE: energy, warmth, passion, determination, transformation. My all-time favorite band is The Doors. You're likely familiar with their iconic song "Light My Fire." This fiery Page may be asking you, "What lights your fire?" Once you know the answer to that question, exploring a fresh new path is as simple as stoking the right flames.

HAT: role, persona, crown chakra. The style of hat worn by the Page of Wands is known as a bowler. The bowler was first created in 1849

in England, when Thomas and William Bowler answered the demand for a fitted, short-crowned hat to wear riding horseback. As the goal of the Page is to eventually evolve into the Knight, the association with riding is notable. In the Wild West, the bowler was even more popular than the cowboy hat, as it was known to survive being blown off even in the strongest gusts of wind. Likewise, it would require a very strong wind to blow out the fiery, creative spark of this Page.

Hats naturally are also associated with the crown chakra due to their location on the head. The crown chakra is the energy center connecting us to the divine, reflecting the spiritual nature of this suit.

PYRAMIDS: spirituality, spiritual ascension, amplification, cosmic energies, desert, fearlessness, mystery, journey, boldness, glorification. The pyramids of Giza (indicated here by the grouping of three pyramids) are a source of great conjecture and mystery, as the true purpose for these massive structures is still debated. One theory from the 1980s known as the Orion correlation theory proposes that the constellation Orion governed their construction. This constellation is mentioned in the Bible several times, but is referred to by the Hebrew word *kesil*, meaning "fool." This takes us back to the very first card of tarot: the Fool. The energy of the Fool is similar to that of the Page of Wands—optimistic, idealistic, and inspired. This association with the stars also reinforces the spiritual nature of this suit as a whole. In simpler terms, the idealistic Page of Wands encourages you to "shoot for the stars."

SALAMANDER: element of fire, renewal, regeneration, transformation.

TUNIC: The yellow color of the Page's tunic is indicative of the warmth and vitality of the sun itself, and this Page brings an energy to the table that can rival that of the sun. Yellow is also the color of the solar plexus chakra, the energetic source of our confidence and self-esteem. Located near the navel, it can be seen as the fire in our belly that motivates and empowers us. The Page of Wands exudes the confidence of youth and harnesses the energy of this chakra.

WAND: element of fire, spiritual realm, masculine principle, life force, energy, growth, vitality, willpower, conduit.

QUICK TAKES: Limitless possibilities; brilliant creative ideas; creative restlessness; exploring new concepts; learning new skills in a creative profession; higher education; a new job offer; feeling called to a new spiritual path; good health and vitality. Good news is coming your way.

REVERSED: *lacking inspiration, lots of great ideas but no follow-through, becoming too easily bored, a rebel without a clue, a bit of bad news.*

Knight of Wands

KEYWORDS: passion, fearlessness, enthusiasm, adventure, impulsiveness, recklessness, arrogance, passive

ASSOCIATIONS

Astrological: Scorpio, Sagittarius

Planetary: none

Elemental: fire

Symbols

ARMOR: protection, shield, preparation, self-preservation, strength, truth, chivalry, honor, mirroring, boundaries. All of the expected noble, chivalrous stuff applies to the armor symbolism in all the Knights of the tarot. But another layer of meaning that can be attributed to the armor in the Knight of Wands is armor has a highly reflective surface that on a spiritual level can act as a mirror of sorts. The Knight of Wands has an enviable lack of fear that we may not feel we possess ourselves. The next time this Knight pops up in a reading, consider the armor representative of looking in a mirror—you have just as much fearlessness as this fiery Knight does.

FEATHER: freedom, travel, ease of movement, change of direction. Combined with the armor symbolism of this card, it's hard not to picture a Roman warrior complete with plumed helmet. The Romans added adornments such as feathers to their helmets to make themselves look taller and more impressive. This type of peacocking energy is perfectly in line with the somewhat cocky energy of the Knight of Wands.

FIRE: energy, warmth, passion, determination, transformation.

GREENERY: abundance, growth.

HORSE: hard work, achievement, status, momentum, movement, freedom, power, solar energy.

PYRAMIDS: spirituality, spiritual ascension, amplification, cosmic energies, desert, fearlessness, mystery, journey, boldness, glorification. While pyramids likely served many purposes, the Egyptians primarily used them as tombs. The Egyptians saw death as the beginning of a great journey to the afterlife. Death was not feared. For the Knight of Wands, the pyramids represent this same spirit of adventure and the ability to venture forth into the unknown without fear.

The Orion correlation theory of the 1980s proposes that the constellation Orion governed the construction of the Giza Pyramids. This association with the stars also reinforces the spiritual nature of this suit as a whole.

SALAMANDER: element of fire, renewal, regeneration, transformation. An interesting tidbit about salamanders is that they do not have any vocal cords. They can make squeaks, clicks, and snaps by exhaling sharply when threatened, but mostly they communicate through touch and chemical signals. As a personality, the fiery, action-based Knight of Wands is not known for being the quiet type. The salamander is a gentle reminder that being hot-headed doesn't always get you ahead. So quench those flames and lower your dang voice.

WAND: element of fire, spiritual realm, masculine principle, life force, energy, growth, vitality, willpower, conduit.

QUICK TAKES: Passionate pursuit of your dreams; a passion project. Charge full speed ahead with an idea; buckle up for a wild ride. Adventurous travel; adrenaline junkie; a passionate lover, a lusty tryst.

REVERSED: *acting impulsively, lacking self-control, being passive in a situation that calls for action, cheating in a relationship, no heat in the bedroom.*

Queen of Wands

KEYWORDS: confidence, vivaciousness, charisma, creativity, sociable, introverted, lacking self-confidence, jealousy

ASSOCIATIONS

Astrological: Pisces, Aries

Planetary: none

Elemental: fire, water

Symbols

CAT: independence, cunningness, magic, divine feminine, protection, luck, solar energy, element of fire. Cats are fascinating creatures for their variety of cultural roles throughout history. They have been both revered and vilified, but in modern times are primarily a beloved domesticated companion. Black cats, in particular, have long been associated with witches, both as a familiar and a shape-shifting form of the witch. This association brings a touch of magic to the table where cats are involved. This Queen embodies a type of creative magic—she can manifest just about anything she imagines. In my mind, this black cat can also be seen as a manifestation of the shadow side of the Queen of Wands. This confident Queen sees the beauty of her own shadow, wisely offering it love and friendship.

The cat also undoubtedly symbolizes Bastet, the Egyptian goddess of home, domesticity, women's secrets, cats, fertility, and childbirth. Cats were revered in ancient Egypt and were considered protectors of the home. Bastet, also known as "Lady of Flame," was a daughter of the sun god Ra and is therefore associated with solar energy and the element of fire. (Just like this fiery Queen.) Interestingly, Bastet was originally depicted as a fierce lioness before she eventually evolved into the cat-headed woman we all know and love. This makes the lion symbol on this card even more relevant. It also presents a fitting duality within the energy of the Queen of Wands. She is a loving and charming woman, but wrong her or someone she cares for and you may just see the ferocious lioness come out.

CROWN: elevation, mastery, power, royalty, sovereignty, authority, intellect, divinity. The crown of the Queen of Wands is adorned with sunflowers, reinforcing her tie to solar and fire energy. As a crown also relates to the crown chakra, the energy center responsible for our connection to spirit, her crown tells us she has a healthy relationship to the divine and her spiritual growth is constantly blooming.

FIRE: energy, warmth, passion, determination, transformation. The charismatic and vivacious nature of the Queen of Wands is like a warm fire that others want to be close to.

LION: strength, courage, instinct, primal, ferocity, desire, passion, sun. The ancient Egyptians had a lion-headed goddess in their pantheon named Sekhmet. Sekhmet was the goddess of war, destruction and healing. Another daughter of the sun god Ra, Sekhmet could be violent and destructive but was also known to heal broken bones, cure disease, and act as the patron of physicians and healers. The vivacious Queen of Wands brings unlimited creative potential to the table. But as Sekhmet illustrates, creation and destruction are two sides of the same coin. There is a quote from Picasso that summarizes the energy of this deck, and I feel it applies to this card as well: "Every act of creation is first an act of destruction."

PYRAMIDS: spirituality, spiritual ascension, amplification, cosmic energies, desert, fearlessness, mystery, journey, boldness, glorification. The extroverted nature of the Queen of Wands is reflected in the pyramids themselves—bold, grand, and impossible to miss.

One potentially relevant theory from the 1980s regarding the Giza Pyramids known as the Orion correlation theory proposes that the constellation Orion governed their construction. This association with the stars also reinforces the spiritual nature of this suit as a whole.

SUNFLOWER: element of fire, association with the sun, association with Leo, confidence, energy, drama, nourishment, devotion. The sunflower is associated with the astrological sign of Leo. Though Leo is not technically the primary sign associated with the Queen of Wands, there is nonetheless a natural correlation due to the personality traits found in the energy of the Queen of Wands. The sunflower also further ties this Queen to the element of fire. One thing I find especially interesting is that the other symbols on the card allude to a dry, desert landscape. If this Queen can make sunflowers grow in an arid climate, she is undoubtedly able to manifest anything she sets her mind to. When this card appears reversed, the energy can indicate jealousy. This harkens back to the Greek sunflower myth of Helios and Clytie. Check your jealousy, lest you do something rash that you'll regret.

WAND: element of fire, spiritual realm, masculine principle, life force, energy, growth, vitality, willpower, conduit.

QUICK TAKES: Be bold in pursuit of your goals, know your worth, be unabashedly yourself, have a lust for life, enjoy socializing and meeting new people, use your natural charm and charisma to influence people, stoke your creative fire. Indicates social engagements, radiant health and vitality.

REVERSED: *rebuild your sense of self-worth, honor your desire for alone time, allowing your shadow side to run the show, jealousy and pettiness, health problems concerning energy levels, frigidity.*

King of Wands

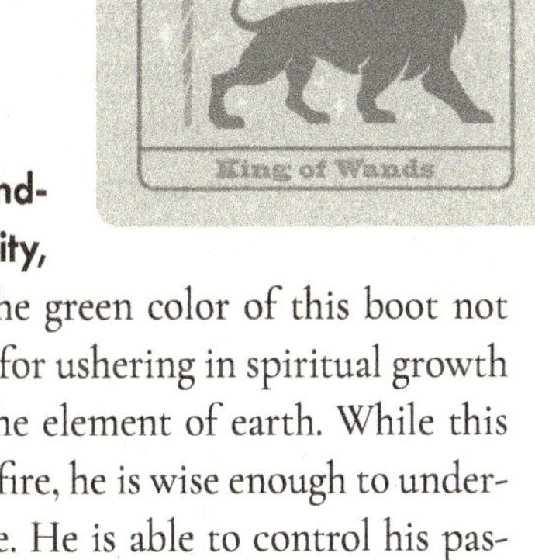

KEYWORDS: leadership, mastermind, visionary, innovation, dynamic, power, dictator, hot-tempered, ineffective

ASSOCIATIONS

Astrological: Cancer, Leo

Planetary: none

Elemental: fire, air

Symbols

BOOT: action, journey, travel, grounding, connection to the earth, humanity, consciousness, civility, protection. The green color of this boot not only symbolizes this King's capacity for ushering in spiritual growth and abundance, it also represents the element of earth. While this King is the master of the element of fire, he is wise enough to understand how other elements affect fire. He is able to control his passions and temper his fiery energy by remaining grounded.

CROWN: elevation, mastery, power, royalty, sovereignty, authority, intellect, divinity. The crown of the King of Wands is embellished with flames, indicating his absolute mastery over the element of fire as well as the spiritual realm that he rules over. A crown is naturally associated with the crown chakra, the energy center responsible for our spiritual nature, so the fire here tells us this King has an abundance of spiritual energy.

FIRE: energy, warmth, passion, determination, transformation.

LION: strength, courage, virility, instinct, primal, ferocity, desire, passion, sun. In addition to the natural symbolic qualities of strength, courage, and virility that this king possesses, there is a link between lions and the Greek god of the sun Apollo. On the island of Delos in Greece there once existed a series of lion sculptures known as the Terrace of the Lions, dedicated to Apollo by the people of Naxos around 600 BCE. This is one of the reasons lions are considered symbols of solar energy. The lion also reinforces this King's tie to the element of fire as well as the astrological sign of Leo.

I also discovered that it's a myth that lions are nocturnal animals. They are, in fact, crepuscular. (Don't worry, I had to look it up to!) That means they are most active during twilight. This is pretty cool because twilight is considered a magical time by many cultures. Professional photographers even refer to it as the "magic hour" due to the beautiful golden light considered perfect for photography. Twilight is neither day nor night; it's the in-between. And it's in this liminal space where creative spark and magic can occur. Thus the lion is a beautiful symbol of the unlimited creative potential this king holds, as well as a positive omen for artists and creators.

SALAMANDER: element of fire, renewal, regeneration, transformation. The alchemists considered salamander more than just a symbol of fire—they were the very *spirit* of fire. Alchemists believed them to have the power to control and manipulate fire without being burned and have the ability to quench fire when necessary. The King of Wands holds this same type of mastery and control over the element of fire.

A bit of medieval lore even credited salamanders with being born from fire. Salamanders like to hide in rotting wood, so it is likely this belief came about when people would throw a log on the fire and little salamanders would scurry out, running for their lives.

WAND: element of fire, spiritual realm, masculine principle, life force, energy, growth, vitality, willpower, conduit. I'll be as tactful as I can here, but a certain saying comes to mind that sums up this King nicely. The confidence and natural leadership this king exudes is "big stick energy," represented by the single, upright wand. (Only swap out "stick" for another word that rhymes, and there you have it.)

QUICK TAKES: The Midas touch; power over any situation; a natural-born leader; boundless physical energy; being in charge; success in business; a big promotion; entrepreneurial ventures; stamina in the bedroom; creating art of any kind.

REVERSED: *power corrupts, a controlling dictator, physical overexertion, inability to control temper.*

Cups

Ace of Cups

KEYWORDS: love, romance, abundance, creativity, intuition, gift, rejection, loss of love, repressed emotions

ASSOCIATIONS

Astrological: all water signs: Cancer, Scorpio, and Pisces

Planetary: none

Elemental: water

Symbols

CLOUD: element of air, silver linings, elevation, dreams, divinity. All of the Aces in the tarot offer a gift or opportunity seemingly "out of the blue." The cloud symbolizes that this gift is divine in nature, heaven sent.

CUP: element of water, emotions, intuition, receptivity, feminine principle.

DOVE: freedom, possibility, ascension, peace, love, messenger, divine feminine, hope. Some of the symbolism associated with doves can be attributed to their very nature. Doves pair up for life and are even known to be affectionate with their mates. This ties beautifully to the love and romance aspects of the Ace of Cups. Multiple gods and goddesses of love have been associated with the dove as well: the Aztec goddess Xochiquetzal, the Mesopotamian goddess Inanna (or Ishtar), the Greek goddess Aphrodite, and the Hindu god Kamadeva. That's a whole lot of potent love energy wrapped up in one bird!

The lovely dove also has a starring role in the Christian story of the great flood and Noah's Ark (which is uncannily similar to a story found in the Mesopotamian Epic of Gilgamesh, which predates the Bible by about 2,000 years). After 40 days, Noah sent the dove out to assess whether dry land was near. It returned with an olive branch (also a symbol of peace), making it forevermore a symbolic messenger of hope, as well as tied not only to the element of air, but also the element of water. (And I can't help but see another layer of symbolism in the fact that the cup in the Ace of Cups is quite literally overflowing with water.)

The Virgin Mary is also depicted with doves quite often, solidifying the symbolic link of the dove to the divine feminine. There is even a belief among some tarot readers that the Ace of Cups predicts the birth of a girl (whereas the Ace of Wands predicts the birth of a boy).

HAND: giving, receiving. All of the Aces in the RWS tarot depict a disembodied hand emerging from the clouds. It represents that a gift of a divine nature is being offered when this card appears. You'll notice that it is a right hand shown. Energetically, the right hand is considered to be the hand that gives energy, and the left hand receives. A gift must be accepted willingly though, and an outstretched hand is what physically accepts a gift that is offered. So the hand also serves as a reminder that it is up to you to take advantage of the gifts and opportunities being offered at this time.

HEART: love. Need I say more?

LOTUS: spiritual awakening, sacredness, purity, resilience, beauty. The lotus grows in swampy conditions, often emerging from the murkiest waters, making it a time-honored symbol of the human spirit's ability to bloom amid the worst conditions. It has been used as a symbol since ancient times: the Buddha and multiple Hindu gods and goddesses are often depicted emerging from a lotus, signifying spiritual awakening. One of these goddesses, Lakshmi, just so happens to be the goddess of good fortune and abundance, both properties ushered in by the Ace of Cups. Her name is derived from the Sanskrit word *laksya*, meaning "aim" or "goal." The Ace of Cups can be a powerful sign of achieving a major goal, particularly in the creative realm.

WAFER: That little circle with the cross on it represents the communion wafer of Christian tradition. The wafer is a symbol of the body of Christ and his ability to be reborn. It reinforces the divine nature of this card as well as the way we may experience an emotional "rebirth" from the joy and love ushered in by the Ace of Cups.

WATER: emotions, life, abundance, movement, ebb and flow, purification, power, depth, intuition, subconscious. In the RWS tarot, there are five distinct, separate streams depicted pouring from the cup. The most common theory I found for this is that the five streams of water represent our five senses. This seems fitting as the love, romance, and creativity hinted at by the Ace of Cups are all experiences that are enriched by our five senses. But the number five is also associated with Mesopotamian Ishtar and Roman Venus, both goddesses of love and sexuality. In England, a knot tied into the form of a pentagram is called a lover's knot. So the presence of five streams adds multiple layers of lovey-dovey goodness to this card.

YOD (י): divinity, spark of creation, building block, beginning, change. There are 26 yods shown on this card. Is this a random smattering of yods or does it have meaning? Well, if you haven't guessed yet, pretty much every little damn thing in the tarot has meaning. The Hebrew name for God (YHWH) has a numerical value of 26. If you assign a numeric value of 1 to 26 to each letter of the alphabet, the letters in the word "God" itself adds up to 26. In the Bible,

Genesis 1:26 speaks of the image of God. I could go on, but you get the gist. The gift heralded by the Ace of Cups is a "god-send."

QUICK TAKES: Love in the purest sense of the word; unconditional love; a new romantic relationship; a soulmate connection; a loving connection with an existing partner; an engagement or wedding; pregnancy or adoption. Your cup "runneth over." Indicates enhanced psychic abilities, creative opportunities, expressing yourself through art, volunteering or charitable giving. Keep an eye out for signs, and nurture your self-love.

REVERSED: *rejection in a relationship, a breakup, an emotionally unavailable partner, repressing your emotions, a need for emotional boundaries.*

2 of Cups

KEYWORDS: love, harmony, emotional balance, compromise, truce, division, separation

ASSOCIATIONS

Astrological: Cancer

Planetary: Venus

Elemental: water

Symbols

CADUCEUS: Also known in Greek mythology as the "staff of Hermes," this signature staff was famously carried by Hermes (Mercury in Roman tradition), god of travel, boundaries, and transitions. This unique staff is also associated with magic and alchemy, representing the transformative potential inherent in the joining of two people.

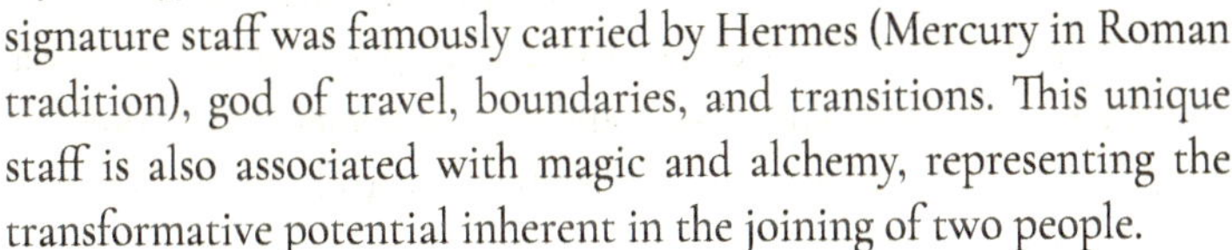

The caduceus symbol was later adopted by the medical profession (possibly having been mistaken for the similar-looking staff of Greek god of healing and medicine, Asclepius), linking it to the attribute of healing. Water (the element of the suit of Cups) has a healing energy to it. A true love connection can indeed be deeply healing to the soul as well.

CUPS: element of water, emotions, intuition, receptivity, feminine principle. The two cups depicted represent two people coming together in some way.

FIRE: energy, warmth, desire, transformation. Fire is one half of an equation (paired with water) that represents the union of two forces coming together to create something new. Fire is the conscious, masculine, passionate side of the equation. It's also worth considering what results from the union of fire and water . . . this pairing has the potential to be a steamy one.

GREEN LANDSCAPE: fertility, abundance, growth.

HOUSE: home, comfort, security, family. I've always loved the expression, "they feel like home to me." The 2 of Cups can signal a true love connection, one that has this potential for this kind of comfort and stability.

LAUREL WREATH: victory, success, triumph, protection, wish fulfillment. There's a sense of victory that comes with finding the perfect partner—especially when you've had some real duds in the past. The harmonious partnership heralded by the 2 of Cups might even be something you've wished for.

LION: In alchemy, the red-winged lion is a symbol of the union of chemicals thought to create the philosopher's stone. This was believed to be a substance that could turn base metals into precious metals like gold or silver. It was also believed to have the power to cure illness.) The chemicals mercury and sulfur turn into a deep red compound when combined to form mercuric sulfide. Many alchemists considered this compound to be the key to the creation of the philosopher's stone. What meaning does this hold for the 2 of Cups? It suggests that the union or partnership that is happening, or soon will, will be a powerful, transformative one.

The winged lion also subtly alludes to the Greek chimera—a monstrous creature that has dominant lion features but is also comprised of several other animals. In the medical world, the term *chimera* refers to a person who has two sets of DNA. This admittedly may be a stretch, but this beautifully illustrates the merging of two into one. It can also be a warning, particularly if this card appears reversed. Be careful not to lose your individual identity within a relationship.

ROSE: passion, vitality, transformation, masculine principle. In Eastern traditions, the rose is linked to the heart chakra. Here, the roses form a crown to be worn on the head, the location of the crown chakra. With the pure love energy of the heart chakra combined with the divinity of the crown chakra, this loving union is bound to be truly divine in nature.

STAGE: fantasy, illusion, overdramatization, perspective, keeping up appearances, story. In the RWS tarot, there are a handful of cards that are illustrated differently than the rest. These cards are sometimes referred to as "stage cards" because the artwork includes a clear demarcation between the landscaped background and the flat foreground, where it appears the characters are standing on a stage. Artist Pamela Colman Smith was active in the world of theater and did a great deal of set design; it's possible this influenced her artwork. Stage cards ask us to take a closer look at the situation at hand, as something may be amiss. With the 2 of Cups, the stage symbol poses questions such as, "Is this partnership or union on the up-and-up?" "Is it really as harmonious as it seems, or is someone pretending?" As with all stage cards, it's up to you to decide if this applies to your situation.

WATER: emotions, life, abundance, ebb and flow, depth. In the 2 of Cups, water is one half of an equation (paired with fire) that represents the union of two forces coming together to create something new. Water is the subconscious, feminine, emotional side of the equation.

QUICK TAKES: A harmonious relationship; a strong alliance; two becoming one; the healing power of love; friendship; a repaired relationship; an engagement or wedding; a strong business partnership; a company merger; a truce after a falling-out.

REVERSED: *separation, end of a relationship, codependency, severed business partnership.*

3 of Cups

KEYWORDS: celebration, friendship, community, joy, antisocial, gossip, overindulgence

ASSOCIATIONS

Astrological: Cancer

Planetary: Mercury

Elemental: water

Symbols

CUPS: element of water, emotions, intuition, receptivity, feminine principle.

FLORAL WREATH: celebration, festivity, victory. The floral wreath is closely linked to the ancient Roman celebration known as Floralia. Floralia was a springtime festival held in honor of the Roman goddess of flowers Flora, at which festivalgoers would wear wreaths made of flowers in their hair and party hard for six straight days. Floralia was known to be quite the pleasure-fest and included lewd performances by partygoers who would shed their clothes when the mood struck them.

GRAPES: abundance, good health, overindulgence, revelry, celebration, blessings, sweetness of life. The grapes here are indicative of the celebration represented by this card. (One that might literally include sharing a bit of wine with friends.) But as grapes can also signify overindulgence, be careful that you don't end up "in your cups." Grapes are also synonymous with Dionysus, god of grapes and wine. With both Flora and Dionysus symbolically in the mix, this celebration is bound to be a rager.

ORANGES: fruitfulness, sweetness, health, joy, success, bitterness. As with the other fruits and vegetables on this card, the oranges add to the sense of celebration. The vibrant color of this juicy gem also links it to the sacral chakra, our energetic pleasure center. The orange's acidic nature can make it occasionally taste bitter or sour. If this card appears reversed, the orange may point to friendships or group dynamics that have soured. Ask yourself, "What can be done to bring back the sweetness?"

PUMPKIN: harvest, nourishment, abundance, strength. All of the fruits and vegetables that appear on this card add to the energy of celebration, as sharing food is a common component of gatherings and celebrations. Pumpkins are also particularly symbolic of the harvest. A great deal of hard work may have led to this moment of joyful celebration. Pumpkins are also incredibly nourishing, just as our friendships can be a source of emotional nourishment. Pumpkins grow in small groups along vines, symbolizing the abundance and joy to be found in close connections.

TRIPLE GODDESS SYMBOL: phases, cycles, divine feminine, magic. The three women portrayed on the RWS 3 of Cups card allude to the three aspects of womanhood embodied in this symbol. the Maiden, the Mother, and the Crone. The presence of the pumpkin, oranges, and grapes, in addition to this symbol's association with Demeter, goddess of the harvest, imparts the symbolic message that we are nourished by our friendships and that there is abundant joy to be found in our time spent with friends. (There is a deeper dive into the triple goddess symbol found on the High Priestess's page.)

QUICK TAKES: Time to celebrate, get together with friends, vacation with friends, have a night out with friends. Let your hair down, let the good times roll. Indicates party planning, reunion with a long lost friend or lover, finding your tribe; new creative ideas; collaboration on a creative project; harmony in body, mind, and spirit.

REVERSED: *out of sync with friends, alone time, a canceled party, overindulging in alcohol or other substances, partying too hard, a third wheel in a relationship, gossip.*

4 of Cups

KEYWORDS: contemplation, selectiveness, boredom, apathy, depression, realignment

ASSOCIATIONS

Astrological: Cancer

Planetary: moon

Elemental: water

Symbols

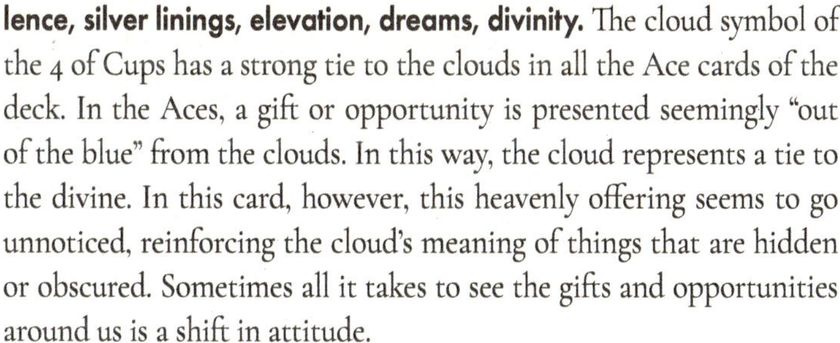

CLOUDS: element of air, thoughts, hidden information, lack of clarity, turbulence, silver linings, elevation, dreams, divinity. The cloud symbol of the 4 of Cups has a strong tie to the clouds in all the Ace cards of the deck. In the Aces, a gift or opportunity is presented seemingly "out of the blue" from the clouds. In this way, the cloud represents a tie to the divine. In this card, however, this heavenly offering seems to go unnoticed, reinforcing the cloud's meaning of things that are hidden or obscured. Sometimes all it takes to see the gifts and opportunities around us is a shift in attitude.

CROSSED ARMS: stubbornness, defensiveness, closed-off.

CUPS: element of water, emotions, intuition, receptivity, feminine principle.

GRASS: elements of earth and water combined, growth, expansion, community, interconnectedness. Given the potential attitude of apathy that accompanies this card, the grass may symbolize that you are not acknowledging the abundance all around you. Also, as you'll never find a single blade of grass growing alone, it may represent that the boredom you feel could be remedied by seeking connection with friends at this time.

TREE: growth, lushness, potential, sustainability, expansion, ascension, time. The specific variety of tree that I've shown here is a weeping willow. Although I couldn't find much evidence that the tree in the RWS version of this card is intended to be a willow, that is what comes to mind when I view this card. (And I apparently am not alone as several other tarot decks have depicted a willow on the 4 of Cups as well.)

The weeping willow is often seen as a symbol of sadness due to its "weeping" branches. But this elegant tree's deeper symbolism is that of flexibility—the branches can bend in outrageous ways without snapping. The 4 of Cups can sometimes indicate a stubborn commitment to apathy or melancholy. The willow suggests the need to be more emotionally flexible and open yourself up to the possibilities around you.

Weeping willows are also known to thrive in wet places, with root systems that actively seek out water. Water is the ruling element of the suit of Cups, representing the emotional realm. Perhaps the willow is also a message to more actively seek out emotional support.

On a more playful note, I can't help but picture the famed Whomping Willow from the Harry Potter series—a particularly violent willow tree that would attack anyone that came near it. Is it possible you've been unnecessarily defensive lately? The 4 of Cups can indicate a certain amount of self-imposed solitude. While quiet contemplation can be a worthy use of time, there's a fine line between enjoyable alone time and melancholy—perhaps it's time you allow people into your space again.

QUICK TAKES: Saying no to opportunities that aren't in alignment to your purpose, turning down invitations and opportunities, ignoring what's right in front of you. Double-check the details; too much of a good thing; feeling sorry for yourself; now is not the time; meditating on what is the best choice for you; social media break.

REVERSED: *hiding from your problems; feeling bored with life; depression; rediscovering your passion; getting back in the game; creating a gratitude practice.*

5 of Cups

KEYWORDS: hopelessness, disappointment, loss, grief, pessimism, peace, gratitude, optimism, healing acceptance

ASSOCIATIONS

Astrological: Scorpio

Planetary: Mars

Elemental: water

Symbols

ARROW: In the RWS tarot, the figure is facing left. I've indicated that direction with a small arrow. Looking to the left symbolizes looking to the past. It may be that the pain of past disappointments still haunts you. The arrow can also indicate that you are spending too much time living in the past. It may be the moment to move on.

BRIDGE: overcoming obstacles, assistance, passage, new direction. The bridge in the 5 of Cups is a beautiful symbolic reminder that, even in our darkest moments, there is always spiritual assistance available to aid us in crossing over from sadness to joy once again.

CASTLE: aspirations, attainment, future reward, comfort, personal domain, refuge, defenses, boundaries, protection. Cups are the suit of the emotional realm. The castle here can symbolize an emotional refuge of sorts. It is a beacon of hope that suggests that, within its walls, you will once again find comfort and an end to the pain, if you choose to willfully move on from your current emotional state.

CLOAK: the emotions we wear, the spiritual realm, protection, journey. The wearer of the cloak in the 5 of Cups is wrapping themselves in the heavy emotions of the current situation. Though their emotional pain is real, the cloak symbolizes that they may also be choosing to wear these difficult emotions for longer than necessary. That cloak will only get heavier (and stinkier) the longer it is worn, but they can choose to shed it and journey on to happier times when they are ready.

CUPS: element of water, emotions, intuition, receptivity, feminine principle. The cups here tell an interesting story. Three of the cups are overturned, spilling out strange liquids, representing loss. Two are still standing, representing that all is not lost and that there is still hope. Essentially, these cups together represent the old proverbial phrase, "is the cup half empty or half full," indicating that the heart of this situation may lie in how you choose to see it.

But what exactly are those strange liquids? As with many things in tarot, the answer is up for debate and speculation. The red liquid could possibly indicate blood or wine. Both can symbolize passion, so the loss may be of a romantic relationship. The green liquid could indicate poison, as some arsenates are naturally green, as is antifreeze, which is dyed green. If it is poison, what you've lost may have been toxic in nature. Perhaps it is a good thing it has spilled. This painful loss may have actually saved you.

STAGE: fantasy, illusion, overdramatization, perspective, story. Stage cards ask us to examine the situation more closely, as there may be more to the story. With the 5 of Cups, the stage symbol brings up the question, "Are things truly as bad as they seem, or is it possible you are overdramatizing things a tad?" As with all stage cards, it's up to you to decide if this applies to your situation or not.

TREE: growth, lushness, potential, sustainability, expansion, ascension, time. The small tree on this card is a symbol of hope—in time this dark night of the soul will pass and you will experience new growth and expansion once again.

WATER: emotions, life, ebb and flow, purification, depth, intuition, subconscious. Water represents our emotions, which can be dark and murky at times. Here, the water can indicate a need to allow the heavy emotions you are experiencing to move on. Water—and emotions—that isn't allowed to flow freely can stagnate. And just as stagnant water can become toxic, so too can our emotions if we don't allow the energy to flow.

QUICK TAKES: Mourning what you've lost; grief over the death of a loved one; loss of a relationship; financial loss or loss of a job; regretting your choices; dwelling on the past; a need to let go of the past and move on; feeling abandoned by someone; seeing the cup as half empty.

REVERSED: *all is not lost, count your blessings, find the silver lining in a difficult situation, finding peace after a time of sadness.*

6 of Cups

KEYWORDS: innocence, joy, childhood, friendship, family, generosity, inner child work, the past

ASSOCIATIONS

Astrological: Scorpio

Planetary: sun

Elemental: water

Symbols

CHILD (represented by small shoes): Innocence, play, truth, boundless energy, generations, memories, inner child work. More than any other card in the deck, this card harnesses all of the symbolic energy of child-like joy and wonder. On a deeper level, this card beckons you to review your relationship with your inner child. Is your inner child healthy and happy, allowing your adult self to approach some situations with a sense of play and wonder? Are there childhood wounds that still need to be examined and addressed? It's possible that both may be true for you. (A great exercise is to choose a particular age that holds meaning for you and write your childhood self a letter. You can let them know they are safe, that something wasn't their fault, or simply offer them unconditional love.)

Another facet of the child symbol on this card is that, in some cases, it can quite literally herald the joyful news of a child coming into your life.

CUPS: element of water, emotions, intuition, receptivity, feminine principle.

FLOWERS: hope, new growth, happiness, beauty, unfolding, renewal, cycles, love. The white color of the flowers found on this card symbolizes innocence. These flowers are also unique in that they have five petals, mimicking the shape of the five-pointed pentagram. The Greeks considered the pentagram a perfect symbol, representing the four elements plus a "fifth element" of spirit that brings a sense of unity to all the others. This symbolism implies that our most loving connections are where we come closest to experiencing a sense of divine perfection.

In my research, I couldn't find any information on what particular flower these white beauties might be, so I decided to come up with a theory of my own. One possible five-petaled white flower is periwinkle. Periwinkle flowers have long been a symbol of hope. In medieval times, there was even a belief that if you smelled this flower while in prison, your jailer would set you free. The presence of a guard on this card (represented by the spear) has always made me feel like the happy children are being guarded and contained in a secure place. While this card still has an overwhelmingly positive vibe to it, it's possible that in the reversed position, a sort of imprisonment is hinted at. As Cups are the suit of the emotional realm, it may suggest emotional imprisonment. The inner child connection of this card implies that when we are wounded from past hurts, it can leave us emotionally stunted or shut down (imprisoned). If that resonates with your situation, take the message of hope that the periwinkle offers and break free from your inner child wounds by seeking out help or methods of healing.

GREENERY: abundance, growth.

HOUSE: home, comfort, security, family.

LIRIPIPE: academic knowledge, silliness. The red hood with a long tail is known as a liripipe. In addition to being a popular item of clothing in medieval times, it has also become associated in modern times with academic achievement, sometimes worn at college graduations. With this card, it can be seen to symbolize the knowledge and understanding to be gained from reflecting on the past. Interestingly, a *liripoop* is a bastardized form of this word meaning a silly person. How perfect is that for a card associated with childhood? Next time you home in on this symbol, consider that it might just be telling you to loosen up and get a little silly.

MITTEN: childhood, innocence, warmth. The mitten is a literal symbol of the "warm and fuzzy" feelings we get when we reminisce about happy times or share precious moments with friends and loved ones. The white color symbolizes the innocence of childhood.

PEDESTAL: elevation, honor, support. One of the cups holds a place of honor upon a pedestal, symbolizing that we should honor our vast emotions as well as where we came from. The pedestal is decorated with an X. When we make an X on a calendar, it means that day is over. The past is over and childhood has ended, but we can still find joy—and sometimes even insight—in occasionally visiting that time in our memories. Just remember not to linger there too long.

SPEAR: guarded, protection, power, masculine principle, sacrifice, imprisonment, targeting. In the RWS tarot, a guard with a spear is seen in the background walking away from the children. Many speculate that this indicates that the children are safe and free to play unhindered. This is one interpretation worth pondering, particularly when you consider the 6 of Cups as a card of past reflection and inner child work. The spear symbolizes that you are safe to connect with your inner child and reminisce about the past. On the other hand, the spear makes me question why these children require this level of guarding in the first place? Is it simply because their lives are precious, indicating that we should be more mindful of valuing and protecting our own inner child? Or are they imprisoned for some reason? Medieval history is rife with children of royal blood being raised under house arrest and guarded heavily when they were considered a threat to the current throne holder. Their lives were likely quite cushy all the same, but the symbolism of imprisonment still fits. In this way, the spear can be seen to symbolize locking away our childhood memories (particularly if trauma was involved) or simply not letting our inner child out to play. Lastly, spears are associated with sacrifice thanks to the stories of both Jesus Christ and Odin. (The Spear of Longinus pierced Jesus's side during the crucifixion and Odin stabbed himself with his own spear, Gungnir, while hanging from the World Tree in order to attain more knowledge.) Perhaps the spear can be seen to represent the sacrifice of innocence we all make in order to enjoy the perks of adulthood, such as advanced wisdom and freedom.

QUICK TAKES: Revisiting happy memories; nostalgic for the good ol' days; connecting with your inner child; embracing a sense of play; reconnecting with childhood friends; returning to your hometown; returning to a previous job; rekindling a relationship with an ex; spending time with siblings; happy parenting dynamics; children in your life; pregnancy or adoption.

REVERSED: *living in the past, too much adulting, leaving home, feeling disconnected from your inner child, seeking guidance with inner child work, emotional imprisonment.*

7 of Cups

KEYWORDS: choices, options, decisions, illusion, imagination, fantasy, overwhelm, clarity

ASSOCIATIONS

Astrological: Scorpio

Planetary: Venus

Elemental: water

CASTLE: aspirations, attainment, future reward, wealth, power, comfort, fantasy, personal domain, public image. Nowhere else in the deck does the castle symbol represent fantasy so keenly. Of all the symbolic options portrayed in the 7 of Cups, the castle may seem like an appealing choice—one that could provide much desired comfort and material security. But the 7 of Cups is a card of illusion and dreaming of what could be (sometimes with no basis in reality). So that castle might be no more than a mirage in the distance. One interesting correlation I found is that this particular castle is associated with the tower of the Tower card as well as the planet of Mars. The Tower card is a place where you definitely don't want to get too cozy.

CLOUDS: element of air, thoughts, hidden information, lack of clarity, silver linings, dreams.

CUPS: element of water, emotions, intuition, receptivity, feminine principle. In this card, each of the seven cups is also associated with a planet or luminary—Sun, Moon, Mercury, Venus, Mars, Jupiter, and Saturn—and with the Major Arcana card associated with them—Strength (dragon), the High Priestess (veiled objecct), the Magician (snake), the Empress (woman), the Tower (castle), the Wheel of Fortune (jewels), and the World (laurel wreath).

DRAGON: risk, dramatic change. While the dragon is a complex symbol, in the case of this card, choosing the dragon may indicate that you are craving powerful and dramatic change in your life. Dragon symbolism varies greatly between different world cultures, ranging from evil to good luck. Choosing the dragon could be a risky gamble. It is also associated with the Sun card.

JEWELS: wealth, status, treasure. The jewels represent a desire for monetary riches and societal status. The saying "all that glitters is not gold" comes to mind. Sure, a little bling may be pretty to look at, but it's doubtful choosing the jewels will bring you any true emotional contentment in life. The jewels are also associated with the Wheel of Fortune card and the planet Jupiter.

LAUREL WREATH: victory, success, triumph, wish fulfillment. The laurel wreath symbolizes that what you desire most at this time is success and achievement. It is also associated with the World card and the planet Saturn.

SNAKE: temptation, earthly realm, sexuality. Of all the choices presented on this card, the snake would be the equivalent of choosing earthly pleasures and carnal desires. It is also associated with the Magician card and the planet Mercury.

VEILED OBJECT: mystery. The 7 of Cups is a card indicating many available options to choose from, but here the veiled object represents something that is hidden from us. It could be something amazing or it could be something pretty lame. It reminds me of the old TV game show *Let's Make a Deal* where a contestant had to make a choice between sticking with the prize that was known or choosing what was "behind door number 2." This symbol is also associated with the High Priestess and the Moon.

WOMAN (represented by the female symbol): beauty, vanity. In the RWS tarot, the head of a beautiful woman is in the cup. I have represented it here simply with the commonly accepted female symbol. Choosing this cup may indicate that what you desire is outer beauty. The lesson of this symbol on the card is to honor your inner beauty first and foremost and beware of narcissism. This symbol is also associated with the Empress card and the planet Venus.

QUICK TAKES: A multitude of options abound; you may choose only one. Wishful thinking; choose carefully; "all that glitters is not gold"; stop fantasizing and take action; smoke and mirrors; discerning reality from fantasy; a need for grounding.

REVERSED: *feeling overwhelmed by multiple opportunities, the choice is clear, choosing not to choose is still a choice.*

8 of Cups

KEYWORDS: dramatic change, abandonment, letting go, moving on, discontent, transition, stagnation, fear of change

ASSOCIATIONS

Astrological: Pisces

Planetary: Saturn

Elemental: water

Symbols

BOOT: action, journey, travel, grounding, connection to the earth, humanity, consciousness. Red is the color of the root chakra, the energy center that governs our sense of security, stability, and survival. This symbolizes that the path you are currently on will lead you to a stable and secure environment. It may also suggest that you need to leave a situation that is threatening your survival.

CLOAK: mystery, the emotions we wear, the spiritual realm, protection, journey. The wearer of the cloak in the 8 of Cups is moving on—to where may be a mystery—but the vibrant red of the cloak suggests they are taking passion, determination, and vitality with them on their journey—a guaranteed recipe for success.

CUPS: element of water, emotions, intuition, receptivity, feminine principle.

ECLIPSE: dramatic change, transformation, emergence, illumination, truth, karma, destiny, revelations. Eclipses are believed to usher in big-time change. The presence of the eclipse on this card suggests that whatever you are letting go of or moving on from is absolutely vital for your growth. Eclipses are also associated with revealing something previously hidden, so if unexpected secrets emerge, know that it is in your best interest that they come to light.

MOUNTAINS: aspiration, courage, challenges, obstacles, retreat, perspective, solitude, ascension. The mountains shown here are steep, suggesting that there may still be difficulties to come. But never forget that the upward ascent of a mountain also represents elevation and striving for loftier ideals. This situation may be challenging, but take heart—the view from the top will be worth it.

ROCK: element of earth, memory, gravity, permanence, rigidity, immovability, unwillingness to change. The rock is in a body of water, indicating that your emotional state might be fraught with rough emotions at this time. The rock can also indicate that you are allowing yourself to stay stuck in a situation when it's time to move on.

STAFF: support, guidance, pilgrimage, solitude, magic, healing. Moving on, particularly to a future that is unknown, can be scary. The staff here suggests that you are divinely supported and guided as you move forward on your journey. We also find a similar staff in the Fool card, suggesting that moving on will require a leap of faith. Additionally, the combination of the staff symbol and eclipse symbol on the 8 of Cups imbues this card with a touch of magic: wherever you are going next has the potential to profoundly transform your life.

WATER: emotions, life, movement, ebb and flow, purification, power, depth, intuition, subconscious. A long time ago I learned a beautiful ritual for letting go. Write down what you want to release on a leaf, then throw it into a river or stream and watch it be carried away with the current. This sentiment is captured perfectly in the water symbol on this card—moving on may be hard but letting go of past disappointments and hurts can allow you to move forward, washed clean of those burdens.

QUICK TAKES: A dramatic change is taking place; leaving an unfulfilling situation; ending an unhappy relationship; leaving an unfulfilling job; knowing when to walk away; leaving behind what no longer serves you; travel.

REVERSED: *drifting aimlessly, avoiding the issue, being afraid to leave an unhappy situation, staying stuck rather than moving on.*

9 of Cups

KEYWORDS: wish fulfillment, abundance, satisfaction, prosperity, success, security, materialism, arrogance, unfulfillment

ASSOCIATIONS

Astrological: Pisces

Planetary: Jupiter

Elemental: water

Symbols

BENCH: contemplation, time-out, pause, patience, foundations. The bench in the 9 of Cups invites you to pause and enjoy the satisfaction and happiness you are currently feeling—or very soon will. This bench is no cushy recliner though; it's hard and flat, and if you sit here too long, it will likely make your butt ache. As Cups are the suit of emotions, this bench reminds us that our feelings are constantly shifting and changing. So enjoy it while it lasts.

CROSSED ARMS: satisfaction, pride, stubbornness, defensiveness. The crossed arms here are less about taking a defiant, angry stance, but rather more about a sense of satisfaction. Abundance and fulfilled wishes often accompany this card. The crossed arms may indicate a desire to defend all that you have acquired. But as water is the element of the suit of Cups, it's important to remember not to try and hold too tightly to abundance, lest it slip right through your hands.

CUPS: element of water, emotions, intuition, receptivity, feminine principle. The nine cups found here are arrayed in an arc, mimicking the rainbow found on the 10 of Cups. This arrangement represents the feelings of joy and hope that accompany abundance.

CURTAIN: hidden information, secrecy. The blue color of the curtain reinforces the element of water and the emotional realm present in this card. It can also represent the old adage "be careful what you wish for," as you really don't know what's behind the curtain.

FEATHER: freedom, hope, change of direction, lightheartedness. The expression "a feather in your cap" signifies an achievement. While the 9 of Cups most definitely indicates an achievement to take pride in, the feather symbol also reminds you to stay lighthearted about your success. Don't take yourself too seriously or that pride could quickly turn to arrogance.

HAT: role, persona, crown chakra. The shape of this particular hat looks a bit like a turban, conjuring images of a genie. The 9 of Cups is known as "the wish card." Perhaps pulling this card is similar to finding a genie in a bottle? Make a wish and see what happens. The red color also indicates passion and drive, indicating that if your wish is to come true, it may require action on your part to make it so.

WHITE CLOTHING: The white color of the clothing represents innocence and purity. It's important to be pure in your intentions when you wish for big things.

QUICK TAKES: Your wish is granted. Unexpected gifts; expressing gratitude; celebrating your success; receiving recognition for your achievements.

REVERSED: *overindulgence and excess, be careful what you wish for, always wanting more, feeling unrecognized, showing off, pride before the fall.*

10 of Cups

KEYWORDS: love, bliss, harmony, family, homecoming, stability, disharmony, dysfunction

ASSOCIATIONS

Astrological: Pisces

Planetary: Mars

Elemental: water

Symbols

CHILD (represented by small shoes): innocence, play, truth, boundless energy, generations, memories, inner child work.

CUPS: element of water, emotions, intuition, receptivity, feminine principle. The cups here mimic the arc of the rainbow, reinforcing the sense of joy and hope found with this card.

GRASS: elements of earth and water combined, growth, expansion, community, interconnectedness.

GREEN LANDSCAPE: fertility, abundance, growth.

HOUSE: home, comfort, security, family.

RAINBOW: joy, hope, bridge, communication, peace, luck. There is so much beauty inherent in the rainbow. The sheer joy we feel when we witness one is present in the blissful energy of the 10 of Cups. As a rainbow appears after a storm, it also indicates that even though you may have gone through tough times recently, you are now entering a happier, more peaceful phase.

Rainbows are also associated with the Greek goddess Iris, whose primary role was messenger of the gods. Iris's link to this symbol reminds us of the importance of open communication, particularly in a marriage or family as indicated in this card.

In Norse mythology, the rainbow bridge (or Bifrost) connects the earthly realm with the realm of the gods. Similarly, some Native American tribes see the rainbow as a bridge between the human and spirit realms. We can view these associations as symbolizing how the emotions of love and bliss connect us to the divine.

STAGE: fantasy, illusion, overdramatization, perspective, keeping up appearances, story. When the stage symbol pops up, it can imply that "all is not what it seems." I have no wish to burst your bubble, but in the case of the 10 of Cups, the stage indicates the possibility that the perfect, idyllic life that is represented may have some cracks in the foundation. As with all stage cards, take the stage with a grain of salt: it may or may not apply. If you sense, however, that it does have some merit, don't fret. The 10 of Cups is such an overwhelmingly positive card that the stage likely only hints at a small hiccup in the situation rather than anything too heavy. Be honest with yourself about what isn't working in your ideal world. It's okay if your life isn't perfect—no one's is.

If this card shows up reversed in a reading, the stage symbol may affirm that someone is trying too hard to keep up appearances. That's understandable since social media bombards us with perfect-looking curated moments that can make us feel like everyone but us has the ideal life, family, relationship, career, etc. Let go of the need to put on an act to impress—you'll find greater satisfaction living an authentic life.

TREE: growth, lushness, potential, sustainability, expansion, ascension, time.

WATER: emotions, life, abundance, movement, ebb and flow, purification, power. The small, peaceful stream in this card indicates that your emotional realm is currently calm. Happiness flows freely, just like the clean water of this stream.

WEDDING RING: marriage, union, eternal bliss.

QUICK TAKES: Happily ever after; your cup runneth over; domestic bliss; a happy family; divine blessings; marriage on the horizon; finding your dream home; moving to the country; ancestral connections; feeling at peace with your life; finding happiness in the little things; generational prosperity.

REVERSED: *discord on the home front, marital problems, dysfunctional family, losing your home, empty-nest syndrome, keeping up appearances.*

Page of Cups

KEYWORDS: creativity, idealism, innocence, curiosity, intuition, sensitivity, surprising insights, good news, repression, lack of confidence, immaturity, bad news

ASSOCIATIONS

Astrological: none

Planetary: none

Elemental: water, earth

Symbols

CUP: element of water, emotions, intuition, receptivity, feminine principle.

FEATHER: freedom, hope, travel, thought, lightheartedness, spiritual evolution, truth. Fans of the 1994 movie *Forrest Gump* will remember the lovely way a drifting feather opens and closes the movie. The Page of Cups embodies the same sense of innocence and idealism that Forrest has. Above all, Forrest is a character who strives to be kind and good in even the most painful of situations. Similarly, this Page's feather reminds us to be our best self no matter where the wind blows us.

FISH: element of water, emotions, feelings, fertility, abundance, state of flow. The fish popping out of the cup represents the surprising insights that sometimes come with this Page. It can also represent a creative idea popping into your mind seemingly from out of nowhere—a bit of divine inspiration.

LOTUS: spiritual awakening, sacredness, purity, resilience, beauty. The lotus grows in swampy conditions, often emerging from the murkiest waters. The idealistic and creative Page has the ability to blossom and create beauty even out of a bad situation. The white color of the lotus also symbolizes the pure heart of the Page of Cups.

SCARF: expression, adornment, flow, comfort, warmth. The blue, flowing scarf of the Page signifies that your emotions and intuition are flowing freely and easily. Scarves are comforting and warming, representing the happier side of the emotional spectrum.

STAGE: fantasy, story. In the case of the Page of Cups, I believe the curtained stage represents the Page's creative brainstorming process—envisioning different scenarios and putting on mini plays in their mind's eye. I mean, there's a fish jumping out of their cup for goodness' sake! This Page clearly enjoys a touch of the fantastical. Creative ideas are all well and good, but without action in the mix, they will only ever live in the realm of fantasy.

WATER: emotions, life, abundance, movement, ebb and flow, purification, power, depth, intuition, subconscious. In addition to all the regular water symbolism pertaining to this Page's suit, I believe another layer of meaning can be attributed here. All the Pages of the tarot are considered to be messengers. I can't help but imagine the powerful waves of the ocean carrying a message in a bottle to a far-off recipient. The practice of sending bottled messages is alleged to have been started by Aristotle's protégé Theophrastus sometime around 310 BCE when he used bottled messages to study ocean currents. They have also been poetically romanticized by the likes of writers such as Edgar Allan Poe and Nicholas Sparks, linking them to the artsy creativity inherent in the Page of Cups.

QUICK TAKES: New creative ideas abound. Believe that anything is possible, be open to new opportunities, explore your creative side, study your emotions. It's okay to be sensitive—approach things with a sense of curiosity, trust your intuition, revamp your personal style. Good news is coming your way.

REVERSED: *stifled creativity, lack of confidence in your creative ideas, doubting your intuition, emotional immaturity, daydreaming without taking action, a bit of bad news.*

Knight of Cups

KEYWORDS: romance, chivalry, loyalty, charm, peacemaker, unpredictability, heartbreak, deception

ASSOCIATIONS

Astrological: Aquarius, Pisces

Planetary: none

Elemental: water, fire

Symbols

ANGEL: blessings, love, divinity, protection, messages. Typically wings in this deck signify angelic energy. But these wings are also associated specifically with Hermes, a messenger god in the Greek pantheon. In the RWS tarot, the wings appear as an embellishment on the Knight's helmet. Hermes is often depicted wearing a similar winged helmet. Like Hermes, this Knight is also a messenger. He brings a message of love and a need for emotional courage. If you've been longing for a romantic relationship, this Knight just might be delivering news that a love connection is on its way or already here.

ARMOR: strength, truth, chivalry, honor, boundaries. All of the expected noble, chivalrous stuff applies to the armor symbolism in the Knights of the tarot. But since the Knight of Cups can also indicate a potential suitor, the armor poses additional questions: What do your energetic boundaries look like at this time? Have you built up your armor so thick due to being emotionally wounded in the past that even true love can't penetrate? Or, alternatively (particularly if this card is in the reverse position), is there a need to reinforce your energetic armor against a charming scoundrel? Developing healthy boundaries is an exercise in balancing what or who to let in and what or who to keep out.

CUP: element of water, emotions, intuition, receptivity, feminine principle.

FISH: element of water, emotions, feelings, fertility, abundance, state of flow.

HORSE: hard work, achievement, status, momentum, movement, freedom, power, solar energy. The white color of this horse, coupled with the symbol of the wings, brings to mind Pegasus, the iconic flying horse of Greek mythology. Pegasus is symbolically linked to all four elements: earth because horses are land-based animals, air because of his ability to fly, water because he could create fountains and springs by stomping his hoof, and fire because he delivered lightning bolts to Zeus. In this way, he symbolizes the emotional harmony and wholeness that is possible when we come from a place of love.

MOUNTAINS: aspiration, courage, challenges, obstacles, retreat, perspective, solitude, ascension.

WATER: emotions, life, abundance, movement, ebb and flow, purification, power, depth, intuition, subconscious.

QUICK TAKES: A romantic suitor, wooing a love interest, an epic date. Be bold in matters of love, a marriage proposal. Unleash your inner artist, take in an art show or play, make heart-led decisions. There is beauty in vulnerability.

REVERSED: *unrequited love, cheating in a relationship, a deceptive charmer, in love with the idea of being in love.*

Queen of Cups

KEYWORDS: compassion, serenity, comfort, nurturing, intuition, dreamer, needy, dependent

ASSOCIATIONS

Astrological: Gemini, Cancer

Planetary: none

Elemental: water

Symbols

ANGEL: blessings, love, divinity, protection, messages.

CIBORIUM: spiritual nourishment, sacredness. A ciborium is a covered metal vessel used in the Catholic mass to hold eucharistic bread. It symbolizes the spiritual nourishment to be found from nurturing relationships.

CROWN: elevation, mastery, power, royalty, sovereignty, authority, divinity. The circular embellishments on the Queen's crown appear in groups of nine. There are nine months in the gestational cycle, which symbolizes this Queen's powerful ability to create—she can nurture anything into existence.

CRYSTAL BALL: intuition, divination, moon energy, guidance. There is no crystal ball shown in the RWS tarot, but the Queen is depicted lovingly gazing at the ciborium she holds with focused intent, almost like looking into a crystal ball to uncover deep mysteries and receive spiritual guidance.

CUP: element of water, emotions, intuition, receptivity, feminine principle.

FISH: element of water, emotions, feelings, fertility, abundance, state of flow. When two circles overlap, the area in the middle makes a fish-like shape known as a *vesica piscis*, an ancient pagan symbol linked to fertility and female sexuality. The vesica piscis is historically associated with the divine feminine and has been called "the womb of the universe." Many goddess incarnations of the sacred feminine share a link to the vesica piscis: Aphrodite, Venus, the Virgin Mary, Ma'at, and Atargatis, to name a few. Let's not beat around the bush (no pun intended): this shape is also keenly reminiscent of the vaginal opening. So it's no wonder all that luscious divine feminine energy is wrapped up in the fish symbol. The nurturing Queen of Cups is similarly dialed in to this divine feminine energy.

LAND: earth element, grounding. The Queen of Cups may be tied to water and the ocean but she still resides on dry land, symbolizing that for all of her dreaminess, she remains emotionally grounded.

MERMAID: emotional depth, finding your voice, feminine principle, dreams, transformation.

ROCKS: element of earth, memory, gravity, permanence, rigidity, immovability, unwillingness to change. Unlike the jagged, rough-edged rocks seen in other cards of this deck, these rocks have been worn smooth by the sea. Similarly, this compassionate Queen can soften even the hardest person with her loving energy. Embrace this Queen's loving nature, especially when dealing with difficult people. The rocks are also stacked, forming a cairn. Cairns are often found marking trailheads to ensure hikers don't lose their way. Similarly, the Queen of Cups reminds us to trust our intuition to guide us on our path.

SEASHELL: feminine principle, intuitive guidance, expansiveness, birth. Many of us have experienced putting our ear up to a shell to hear the sounds of the ocean. The vast, watery depths of the sea symbolize our subconscious thoughts and deepest emotions. The seashell symbol nudges us to listen to our own intuitive guidance. Shells also continue to expand throughout a mollusk's life to allow for growth. In this same way, this card can indicate expansion. Scallop shells are associated with both Venus and Lakshmi. The famous painting *Birth of Venus* by Botticelli depicts the goddess being born out of the ocean in a large scallop shell. Venus is the goddess of love, beauty, and fertility—all qualities showcased in this card. This depiction also symbolizes the birth of great things in your life. Lakshmi, a Hindu goddess, is known to transform dreams into reality—a fitting association for the Queen of Cups.

WATER: emotions, life, abundance, movement, ebb and flow, purification, power, depth, intuition, subconscious.

QUICK TAKES: Powerful intuitive abilities. Trust your inner voice, nurture your self-love, be an emotional support for others. Indicates healing and counseling professions. Seek out a counselor or therapist, be in flow with natural cycles, create art intuitively.

REVERSED: *emotional instability, feeling emotionally drained, ignoring your intuition, being too clingy or needy.*

King of Cups

KEYWORDS: wisdom, maturity, empathy, diplomacy, balance, creativity, generosity, manipulation, self-centric, overreaction

ASSOCIATIONS

Astrological: Libra, Scorpio

Planetary: none

Elemental: water, air

Symbols

BOAT: navigation, inner compass. The boat symbolizes this King's mastery of the emotional realm and his ability to navigate life's rough patches with ease.

CROWN: elevation, mastery, power, royalty, sovereignty, authority, intellect, divinity. The watery-looking crown of the King of Cups reinforces his mastery over the realm of emotions.

CUP: element of water, emotions, intuition, receptivity, feminine principle.

DOLPHIN: communication, intelligence, play, balance, help, psychic abilities, transformation. Dolphins embody the elements of both water and air—they live in the water but, as mammals, require air to survive. This symbolizes the ability of the King of Cups to balance the emotional and intellectual realms. There are also numerous accounts of dolphins helping humans in perilous conditions at sea. This King has a similar empathetic nature and thrives in his role as emotional support for others.

FISH: element of water, emotions, feelings, fertility, abundance, state of flow.

SCEPTER: power, royalty, authority. The scepter of the King of Cups is topped with a lotus flower. In Hinduism, the god Vishnu is often portrayed holding a lotus in one of his many hands. Vishnu is the preserver of balance and order and upholds universal law. Known to have a gentle and merciful nature, Vishnu perfectly symbolizes the diplomacy and balance present in the King of Cups.

SNAKE: renewal, fertility, earthly realm. The RWS tarot does not show a literal snake on this card. But the King's unique shoes appear to be made of some green, scaly material—possibly snakeskin. The snake symbol implies that this wise King grounds his emotions and creativity in the earthly realm in order to be successful. It also hints at the renewing properties of water, this King's primary governing element.

WATER: emotions, life, abundance, movement, ebb and flow, purification, power, depth, intuition, subconscious. The choppy waters of the King of Cups indicate turbulent emotions. This serves to highlight the King's mastery of the emotional realm: he can navigate these rough emotional waters like a boss.

WHALE: wisdom, psychic abilities, magnificence, emotional depths.

QUICK TAKES: A balanced approach between the heart and the head, mastery over one's emotions, a need for diplomacy, divine masculine energy, wise counsel, ability to read the room, rise above the drama, explore creative interests, charitable works.

REVERSED: *emotional drama, emotional manipulation.*

Swords

Ace of Swords

KEYWORDS: clarity, epiphany, truth, breakthrough, new ideas, opportunity, overthinking, confusion, irrational

ASSOCIATIONS

Astrological: all air signs—Gemini, Libra, and Aquarius

Planetary: none

Elemental: air

Symbols

CLOUDS: element of air, silver linings, elevation, dreams, divinity. All of the Aces in the tarot offer a gift or opportunity seemingly "out of the blue." The cloud symbolizes that this gift is divine in nature, heaven sent.

CROWN: elevation, mastery, power, sovereignty, authority, intellect, divinity. Since crowns are an adornment for the head (location of the good ol' wrinkly brain) there is a natural association here with the mental realm and the intellect that the Ace of Swords relates to. Interestingly, the Ace of Swords is the only Ace in the deck that includes a crown. When you view this symbol on this card, think of it as indicating mental elevation.

HAND: giving, receiving. All of the Aces in the RWS tarot depict a disembodied hand emerging from the clouds. It represents that a gift of a divine nature is being offered when this card appears. You'll notice that a right hand is shown. Energetically, the right hand is considered to be the hand that gives energy, and the left hand receives. A gift must be accepted willingly, though, and an outstretched hand is what physically accepts a gift that is offered. So the hand also serves as a reminder that it is up to you to take advantage of the gifts and opportunities being offered to you at this time.

LAUREL: victory, success, triumph, higher learning, wish fulfillment. There is some debate about the identity of the two plants depicted on the Ace of Swords in the RWS tarot. Laurel is one possibility and, in my opinion, spot-on symbolically. One of laurel's meanings is higher learning, a perfect attribute to pair with the intellectual realm of the Swords suit. Aces come bearing a gift or opportunity, which ties beautifully to laurel's wish fulfillment. Laurel is also associated with the Greek god Apollo. Apollo is known as the god of truth (among about a dozen other things), and the Ace of Swords is sometimes referred to as the "sword of truth." Isn't that just the chef's kiss of perfection?

MOUNTAINS: aspiration, courage, challenges, obstacles, retreat, perspective, solitude, ascension. The Ace of Swords is a card of truth. Getting to the truth of a matter can be liberating, but the truth can also be difficult to face. The sharp mountains of the Ace of Swords reflect that the mental journey through the suit of Swords initiated here may hold some tough challenges along the way.

OLIVES: peace, victory, wisdom, longevity, health. Olives are associated with the Greek goddess Athena, who competed with Poseidon for possession of the city that would come to be named Athens. (Want to guess who won?) Poseidon offered a salt spring and Athena offered a date palm tree. The people chose Athena's gift, as hers was a source of food. Athena just so happens to be the goddess of wisdom, an apt association for the Ace of Swords. Because of this myth, olives are also a symbol of victory. We can consider truth prevailing as a victory over mental deception. Olives are also an attribute of Eirene, the Greek goddess of peace, signifying the peace that comes from accepting the truth.

A single olive tree can live and produce fruit for an average of 500 years, making it a symbol of longevity and health. An inspired, active mind, as represented by the Ace of Swords, contributes to the longevity of our mental health.

PALM: wisdom, abundance, hope, victory. There are two plants shown on the RWS Ace of Swords card, but it is widely debated what each is. One of the plants is believed to be either laurel (already discussed) or palm. I have included both in my card as I believe they both are apt symbols for the energy here. Palm leaves are associated with the Greek goddess of victory Nike. Nike is an aspect of the goddess Athena, who just happens to be the goddess of wisdom—a perfect representation for the Ace of Swords. Nike is also the only winged goddess in the Greek pantheon, reinforcing the element of air represented by the suit of Swords.

As early as 500 BCE, people from the Middle East to the Far East used palm leaves as "paper" to write down their stories and thoughts. This is representative of this Ace's properties of communication, speaking your truth, and elevated thinking. As the Aces also indicate new ideas in the mental realm, this is a wonderful omen for writers or those wishing to write a book.

SWORD: element of air, intellect, power, discernment, decisiveness, truth, impartiality, purification, finality. This sword is known as "the sword of truth." Its double-edged blade has the ability to swiftly cut through any deceptions, providing total mental clarity.

YOD (י): divinity, spark of creation, building block, beginning, change. Yod is the 10th letter of the Hebrew alphabet. Numerologically, 10 breaks down to 1 (1 + 0 = 1). The Ace is the first card of the suit of Swords and ushers in a new beginning. The spark of creation represented by the yod symbolizes the first hint of inspiration that leads to new ideas.

QUICK TAKES: An aha moment, new fresh ideas, much-needed clarity on a situation, clear communication, speaking your truth, cutting through the bullshit, being intentional with your thinking, a new job opportunity, a successful surgery.

REVERSED: *clouded judgment, miscommunication, overthinking a problem, allowing irrational thoughts to rule your mind, reacting emotionally in a situation where logic is needed.*

2 of Swords

KEYWORDS: balance, contemplation, difficult decisions, clarity, denial, stress, indecision, avoidance, stalemate, clarity

ASSOCIATIONS

Astrological: Libra

Planetary: moon

Elemental: air

Symbols

BENCH: contemplation, time-out, pause, patience, foundations. When you find yourself facing a difficult situation, the bench metaphorically invites you to slow down and take a load off so that you may find clarity. The act of sitting suggests a sense of calm. When combined with the blindfold symbol, I envision someone deep in a meditative state—exactly the type of still energy needed to find the answer within.

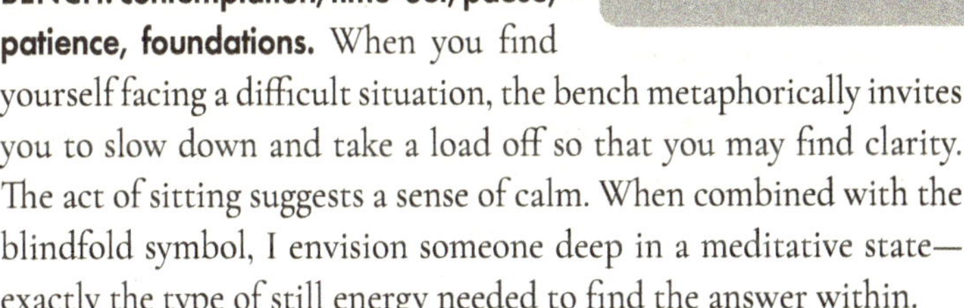

BLINDFOLD: hidden information, lack of clarity, denial, avoidance. The blindfold symbol in the 2 of Swords may represent that you are missing critical information needed to make a clear decision. On the flip side of that, it can also symbolize that you are willfully "putting blinders on" in order to avoid making a difficult decision.

MOON: intuition, the subconscious, shadow work, reflection, hidden information. The moon in the 2 of Swords is indicative of the need to journey inward to find the answers you seek. It can also suggest that there is information hidden to you at this time—a symbolic meaning supported by the blindfold.

ROCK: element of earth, memory, gravity, permanence, rigidity, immovability, unwillingness to change. The rock symbolizes an unwillingness to make a decision, particularly if this card appears reversed. The water surrounding the rock indicates that the situation will continue forward, whether you make a decision or not. Remember, stubbornly refusing to choose is also a choice.

STAGE: fantasy, illusion, overdramatization, perspective, story. Sometimes when the stage symbol appears, the focus is less about putting on an act for others and more about overdramatizing a situation in our own head. It can be indicative of the stories we tell ourselves. With the 2 of Swords, the stage symbol begs the question, "Does this decision really need to be as stressful as you're making it, or is it possible you're building it up to be more dramatic than it needs to be?"

SWORDS: element of air, intellect, power, discernment, decisiveness, truth, impartiality, purification, finality.

WATER: emotions, life, movement, ebb and flow, purification, power, depth, intuition, subconscious. The tranquil water found on this card signals that the wisdom tucked deep away within our subconscious is best found through stillness and calm.

QUICK TAKES: Weigh your options. Torn between two possible choices, more information is needed to make an informed decision. Indicates the need to make a difficult decision, meditate to find the answer you seek. A compromise brings balance; play the role of peacekeeper. Vision problems.

REVERSED: *a stalemate, avoiding making a difficult choice, an end to a conflict, the blinders come off and you can clearly see which choice to make.*

3 of Swords

KEYWORDS: heartbreak, sorrow, depression, breakup, self-deprecation, optimism, recovery

ASSOCIATIONS

Astrological: Libra

Planetary: Saturn

Elemental: air

Symbols

CLOUDS: element of air, thoughts, constancy of change, turbulence, silver linings. The gray rain clouds of the 3 of Swords signify the gloomy mood that accompanies heartache and sorrow. Have you ever been so down in the dumps that even on a sunny day it felt like you had your own personal rain cloud following you around? That's the mood of the 3 of Swords. There may be no quick cure for these types of emotion, but you can take heart in the fact that the ever-changing nature of clouds ensures this heaviness will move on soon enough. In the case of a breakup, almost all of us have had a relationship that, in hindsight, we realize we are so much better off without. So keep in mind these dark clouds may just have a silver lining.

HEART: love, romance, sexuality, consciousness, soul. Ah, the beloved heart . . . quite possibly one of the most widely used and easily identifiable symbols in the world. But have you ever pondered why this iconic heart looks very little like an actual heart? It's likely the shape was inspired by a species of now extinct giant fennel called silphium. Silphium was used by the ancient Greeks and Romans as a form of birth control. It grew particularly plentiful in the North African colony of Cyrene, where for a time it was even stamped on their coins. Love and sex—they go together like peas and carrots and are responsible for the most blissful sensations in the human experience, so it's no surprise this sought-after plant became emblematic of the heart. Since the heart shown here appears pierced, all of the yummy bliss associated with love and sex gets energetically turned on its head, resulting in the painful emotion of heartache.

We all know the heart for its association with love and emotions. But some big-name historical figures such as Aristotle actually believed the heart to be the seat of our consciousness and intellect. This is an apt association for this card since Swords are the suit of the intellectual realm. In this way, the pierced heart symbolizes the dark thoughts that accompany heartbreak as well as the potential for steering our thoughts back to a more positive place.

RAIN: sadness, melancholy, foreboding, cleansing. The raindrops seen here can just as easily be interpreted as the tears that come with heartbreak. Rain and tears share a beautiful common thread—they are both cleansing.

SWORDS: element of air, intellect, power, discernment, decisiveness, truth, impartiality, purification, finality. As Swords are the suit of the mental realm, they are naturally symbolic of our thoughts. Just as our thoughts manifest into the words we speak, the sword conjures up a slew of themes around communication. While it's worthwhile to be blunt and truthful when we speak, we must also remember that words are weapons that can wound and should be wielded with care, lest we cause the kind of piercing heartache the 3 of Swords suggests.

QUICK TAKES: Deeply hurt feelings, a breakup or divorce, hurtful words cut to the core, being bullied, a reminder that this too shall pass, medical concerns dealing with the heart. Allow yourself a good cry in order to move on.

REVERSED: *hurting yourself with negative self-talk, being too thin-skinned, your heartache is nearing an end, recovering from a painful breakup, positive thinking leads to a happier time, physical healing.*

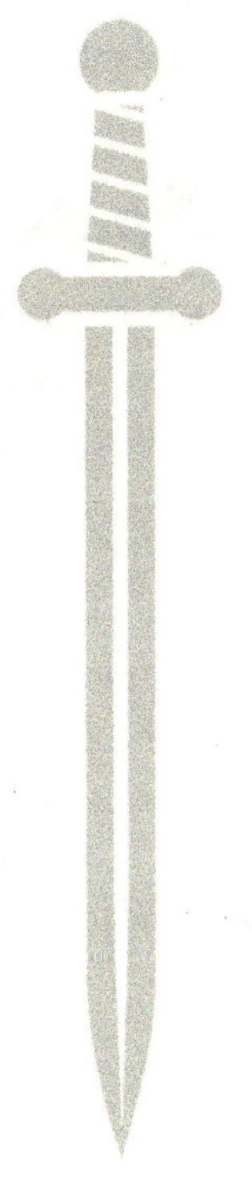

4 of Swords

KEYWORDS: rest, rejuvenation, retreat, contemplation, stress, exhaustion, anxiety, restlessness

ASSOCIATIONS

Astrological: Libra

Planetary: Jupiter

Elemental: air

Symbols

ARMOR: protection, shield, strength, self-preservation, preparation, boundaries. With the 4 of Swords being a card of deep rest, it may seem odd that armor—indicative of a battle—is present. This card may indicate that the individual has recently been engaged in a great battle and now needs to recharge. But I believe a deeper meaning to the armor symbol is at play here. Armor also represents boundaries, so it's worth asking yourself if the need for such deep rest has been brought on by the inability to say no and taking on more than you can handle. Learning to say no to some things is an incredibly powerful way to reinforce your boundaries and avoid burnout.

PAX: peace. Though this is more of a word than a symbol, it felt important to include in this card. In the RWS tarot, *PAX* appears in the scene of the stained-glass window. *Pax* is the Latin word for "peace." The Roman pantheon also includes a goddess by that name. She is the goddess of . . . you guessed it . . . peace. The word also holds a place in the Catholic Mass in the phrases *pax vobis* (peace to you) and *pax vobiscum* (peace with you). To sum it up, this word embodies the spirit-renewing sense of peace that we are able to find when we allow ourselves to slow down, rest, and even isolate for a time.

PILLOW: rest. I chose to add this fluffy little pillow to reinforce this card's association with rest.

PRAYER HANDS: devotion, homage, divine communication, surrender, respect, gratitude, unity, heart opening, purity. As art history will tell us, this positioning of hands is several thousand years old. Prayer hands appear in a variety of religions and cultures. In Christianity, it is a common pose of supplication. One sweet explanation I found described a child being told that the fingers point up so that the prayers will travel to heaven. However, this hand position is not limited to the Christian religion. You can walk into any yoga studio and find people holding their hands together and saying "namaste." This practice originated in India several thousand years ago as a form of greeting intended to show respect and gratitude. This Sanskrit term translates to "the divine in me bows to the same divine in you." Both prayer and yoga carry the energy of slowing down, quiet contemplation, and a marked sense of peace that comes from connecting to the divine—all qualities brought to the table by the 4 of Swords.

Another interesting use of this hand gesture dates back to ancient Rome, when a prisoner's hands were brought together to be bound. A captured soldier could avoid immediate death simply by joining their hands together as a way of saying "I surrender." Many of us struggle with allowing ourselves to slow down and recharge. The prayer hands can be seen as symbolic of surrendering to a state of deep rest.

STAINED-GLASS WINDOW: hope, sanctuary, grandiosity, inspiration, renewal, storytelling. Stained-glass windows are most often found in churches. Churches are places where we sit still, speak in whispers, and pray (a form of meditation for all practical purposes). This card encourages you to embrace all of those habits for a time in order to recharge and renew.

SWORDS: element of air, intellect, power, discernment, decisiveness, truth, impartiality, purification, finality. You'll notice that the bottom sword points to the left. In tarot, the left is the direction of the past. Likely, the need for recharging and rest has stemmed from the challenges of the recent past. While it's never advised to dwell on the past too long, in this case the left-pointing sword is telling you that it may be beneficial to spend a little time contemplating recent events in order to process and learn from them.

TOMB: death, stillness. Long ago, this card was associated with a literal death, but that is not typically the case in modern times. This card is about a need for deep rest, particularly after a stressful time. When I see the tomb on this card, I think of the expression "sleep like the dead." That is the type of deep rest this card is nudging you toward.

QUICK TAKES: Time to recharge your battery—a solo retreat or vacation, a time-out is necessary, take a mental health day from work. Indicates the rejuvenating power of deep rest, meditation, or a power nap.

REVERSED: *burnout to the point of exhaustion, feeling pressured to always be doing something, ignoring your need for rest, stress-induced insomnia, sickness brought on by overwork, being quarantined, time to get back to work.*

5 of Swords

KEYWORDS: competition, aggression, discord, defeat, reconciliation, truce, peace

ASSOCIATIONS

Astrological: Aquarius

Planetary: Venus

Elemental: air

Symbols

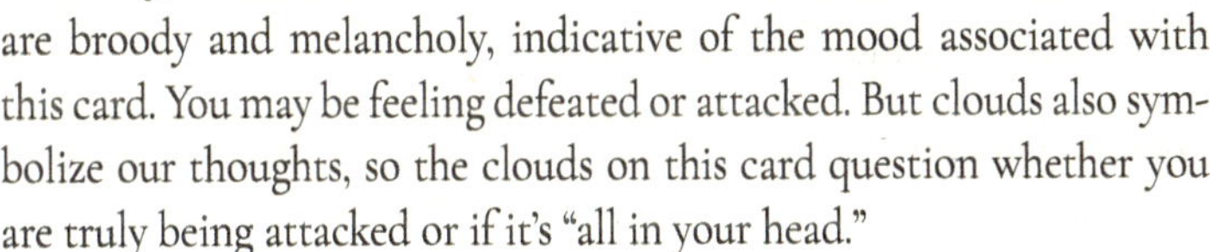

CLOUDS: element of air, thoughts, lack of clarity, turbulence. The clouds here are broody and melancholy, indicative of the mood associated with this card. You may be feeling defeated or attacked. But clouds also symbolize our thoughts, so the clouds on this card question whether you are truly being attacked or if it's "all in your head."

MOUNTAINS: courage, challenges, obstacles, perspective, solitude. The jagged mountains lean to the left. In tarot, left is typically the direction associated with the past. The struggles of this situation may have been great, but they have mostly passed now. Don't dwell on the past with bitterness. Whether you're the defeated or the victor, it's time to move on, preferably with forgiveness in your heart.

STAGE: fantasy, illusion, overdramatization, perspective, story. Have you ever met someone who claims to despise drama but thrives on it nonetheless? That's the vibe I get from the stage symbol on this card. The 5 of Swords indicates the end of a battle —whether you have emerged victorious or been defeated may be irrelevant because the stage symbol poses the question of whether this battle was even necessary to begin with. We are all guilty at times of inventing little micro-dramas in our head; the stage reminds us to save the drama for when it's truly warranted.

SWORDS: element of air, intellect, power, discernment, decisiveness, truth, impartiality, purification, finality.

TUNIC: growth, renewal, and healing. The 5 of Swords is a card of conflict, but the green tunic indicates that once the battle has passed, it may be possible for all parties involved to find healing and growth from this situation.

Green is also notorious for being the color of jealousy. In Shakespeare's play *Othello*, Iago says, "O beware, my lord, of jealousy; It is the green-eyed monster." The green tunic asks you to assess your involvement in this conflict. Are you the victim here, or have you brought your own green-eyed monster to the table?

Green is also the color associated with the heart chakra, our energetic center of love. When your heart chakra is balanced, you'll find it a bit easier to find forgiveness in your heart.

WATER: emotions, movement, ebb and flow, depth, intuition, subconscious. The body of water here is calm but deep, suggesting that though you may feel a sense of defeat or acceptance from a recent conflict, there are more emotions under the surface to explore. The natural ebb and flow of water also indicates that the tides could very soon shift and be tumultuous once again, so prepare yourself for the fact that this conflict may not be over.

QUICK TAKES: Feeling defeated. Choose your battles wisely. Indicates a bitter loss, acting aggressively, poor sportsmanship, winning at any cost, playing dirty, deceitful or untrustworthy person, a bully, dirty office politics, theft of personal belongings, constant bickering in a relationship. Know when to walk away and cut your losses.

REVERSED: *a peaceful end to a conflict, lies exposed, waving the white flag, knowing when to surrender, accepting defeat with grace.*

6 of Swords

KEYWORDS: transition, release, moving on, healing, calm, stuck, stagnation, escapism

ASSOCIATIONS

Astrological: Aquarius

Planetary: Mercury

Elemental: air

Symbols

BANDAGE: wound, injury, emotional pain, struggle, healing. The bandage indicates that the situation you are moving on from may have left you feeling emotionally, mentally, or even physically beat-up.

If you'll allow me to get "sciency" for a moment, the human body is really a remarkable wonder. Our cells are constantly regenerating and replacing themselves with new ones. In fact, research has shown that the body literally replaces the majority of itself with a new set of cells every seven to ten years. How cool is that?! When you get a small cut, the body immediately begins to repair itself. Though this process takes time and can be painful, the body's built-in ability to know exactly what to do is endlessly fascinating to me. We wisely use bandages to protect a healing wound from dirt and bacteria, but really the body is doing 90 percent of the work for us, forming a nice crusty scab to protect the wound as it heals. I feel that our spirit is also capable of this same level of self-healing under the right conditions. So when you see the bandage symbol, my hope is that it will not only convey some of the hardship of the situation, but also a sense of hope for the renewal and healing to come.

BOAT: journey, transition, refuge. Boats represent a certain level of safety, as a sturdy vessel can protect a traveler from the perils of the chaotic sea. A boat can also symbolize the transition to a safe haven when there is a need to leave an unhealthy situation.

CHILD (REPRESENTED BY SMALL SHOES): innocence, truth, generations, memories, inner child work. The child symbol of the 6 of Swords has a less playful energy than it has when it appears in other cards. A parental figure accompanies it in the symbol of the cloak, as well as a boat operator, so there is comfort in the fact this child is not alone. But the journey they are on has a hint of sadness to it—this child may not be able to enjoy the carefree joy attributed to childhood at this time. The innocence that the child symbolizes is in some ways even more profound here. It shares a message that no matter what dark times we experience, our spirit remains innocent and pure. We can choose to embrace this idea by willfully refusing to allow our experiences to make us bitter or jaded, and instead continue to believe in the good of the world—no matter how deeply we've been hurt.

CLOAK: concealment, mystery, the emotions we wear, the spiritual realm, protection, journey. The cloak of the 6 of Swords is the only one in the deck that is shown with the hood up and the back turned toward us, indicating a total concealment. Symbolically, this can represent the need to leave a bad situation in a covert way. (I can't help but think of victims of domestic abuse here, particularly with the child represented as well.) But a less heavy interpretation also exists: moving on from a bad situation of your own making, thus the desire to slink away unnoticed. No matter what has instigated this journey, you can take comfort in the fact that the cloak also symbolizes that you are divinely protected as you move forward to a better situation.

SWORDS: element of air, intellect, power, discernment, decisiveness, truth, impartiality, purification, finality.

WATER: emotions, life, abundance, movement, ebb and flow, purification, power, depth, intuition, subconscious. I love that there are two types of water depicted on this card. Together they bear a message of hope: you may be coming out of a rough time, but take heart—there are peaceful waters just ahead.

QUICK TAKES: A fresh start, overcoming hardship, moving on from a relationship or job, leaving behind what no longer serves you, escaping a bad situation, heading toward calmer waters, learning tough life lessons, physical healing and recovery, traveling overseas, domestic abuse.

REVERSED: *running away from your problems, resisting change, feeling trapped or stuck, holding on to the past, a storm is coming, inner child work.*

7 of Swords

KEYWORDS: theft, deception, dishonesty, cunning, trickery, confessions, secrets

ASSOCIATIONS

Astrological: Aquarius

Planetary: moon

Elemental: air

Symbols

BLINDFOLD: hidden information, lack of clarity, denial, avoidance, lack of foresight. Though there is no literal blindfold depicted in the RWS 7 of Swords card, the person's eyes are closed, alluding to a certain sense of nonseeing. As this card can be a card of deception (and even theft), the blindfold may indicate that you are "blind" to potential trickery and deceit being enacted by someone around you. Alternatively, if you are the one attempting to be a sneaky snake, the blindfold may represent that you do not have the foresight to see how poor choices made now may affect your future.

BOOT: action, journey, travel, grounding, connection to the earth, humanity, consciousness, civility, protection. This boot is depicted on its tippy-toe, indicating that someone is attempting to sneak around in this situation. The boot asks: "Are you the sneaky one? Or is it someone around you?"

CAMPFIRE: energy, warmth, camaraderie, happiness. For most of us, the image of a campfire evokes memories of shared time and warm, happy camaraderie with friends or family. The campfire suggests that those gathered around it have no idea that they are being deceived—possibly even by someone in their close circle.

FLAG: attention, signal, authority, victory, affiliation. The flag of the 7 of Swords is less about making a proclamation and more about asking where your allegiances lie. If you are the one being deceptive, it's possible you're not even being true to yourself and any sense of victory you feel in this situation is hollow. If the deception is coming from another, this flag is a big ol' signal flapping in the wind that someone has betrayed your alliance.

PORCUPINE: danger, caution, discernment, self-defense. There is no porcupine shown in the RWS version of this card—this is an inclusion of my own choosing. But the primary figure wears a hat with a prickly looking black rim that reminds me of a porcupine. And it's a rather apt symbol for this card. Porcupines are known for their ability to defend themselves but are peaceful and passive in nature. In fact, they prefer to keep their quills flat until they feel threatened. So when you see a porcupine with its quills splayed out, such as on this card, you know there's a threat lurking nearby. You may not be aware of the danger around you yet, but this porcupine is telling you to get those quills up and be on the defense. Porcupines also mate for life, but the females are very picky about the mate they choose. This porcupine symbol may also serve as a warning to be more discerning about your own choice of mate, particularly if you've been wronged in the past.

STAGE: fantasy, illusion, perspective, story. When a stage card pops up, it invites us to take a closer look at what might really be going on with a situation. All may not be what it seems, and in the case of the 7 of Swords, the stage reinforces the card's energy of deception and trickery. Be on guard: someone may be smiling to your face while scheming behind your back.

SWORDS: element of air, intellect, power, discernment, decisiveness, truth, impartiality, purification, finality. The swords here appear in a group of five and a group of two. The five swords mirror the conflict and aggression of the 5 of Swords card. There is also an element of conflict here, but it is more subtle than the energy of the 5 of Swords. Here it is underhanded, deceptive, and secret in nature. The two swords indicate something left behind. They can be seen to represent evidence of treachery that will lead to the culprit being discovered.

TENT: temporary, impermanence, shelter, performance, home. In the RWS 7 of Swords, the tents are believed to be part of a military encampment that a figure is sneaking away from with five stolen swords in tow. Another interpretation is that they are part of something like a Middle Eastern bazaar—an open-air marketplace full of shops. The theme of thievery works just as well with this interpretation. To me though, the colorful tents remind me of a circus. And a major component of a circus is the performance being put on. This is fittingly symbolic of someone putting on a show to your face while deceiving you behind your back. I also find the tent an interesting symbol for its impermanence. Sadly, when this card pops up, it can indicate a temporary relationship without a strong foundation—one that ends once their deception comes to light.

QUICK TAKES: Theft of property or ideas, acting deceptively or a deceptive person, sneaking around behind someone's back, a need to fly under the radar. Be careful who you share private information with. Indicates plagiarism, giving poor effort, getting away with something you know to be wrong, someone pretending to be your friend, criminal actions, a strategic plan.

REVERSED: *impostor syndrome, keeping secrets from others, being caught red-handed, coming clean.*

8 of Swords

KEYWORDS: negativity, restriction, helplessness, victim mentality, freedom, empowerment

ASSOCIATIONS

Astrological: Gemini

Planetary: Jupiter

Elemental: air

BLINDFOLD: hidden information, lack of clarity, victim mentality, denial, close-mindedness, avoidance. The suit of Swords is linked to the mental realm, and the blindfold here symbolizes an unwillingness to envision a way forward from your current situation due to negative thinking. To take this idea a little further: when we feed our mind a continuous diet of negative thoughts, we become "blind" to the myriad things we have to be grateful for, thus keeping us stuck in the muck.

CASTLE: comfort, personal domain, refuge, defenses, boundaries, protection. With the "stuck" energy of this card, the castle represents a potential sanctuary from the current situation. But it's possible negative thinking is blinding you to solutions that are within your reach.

CLOUD: element of air, thoughts, hidden information, lack of clarity, turbulence. Just as clouds can obscure our vision, the overcast energy of this card suggests that we are not seeing the truth with clarity. Clouds are also symbolic of our thoughts. In the case of the 8 of Swords, limiting beliefs and negative thought patterns may be "clouding our vision" from seeing the potential solutions nearby.

MOUNTAIN: aspiration, courage, challenges, obstacles, retreat, perspective, solitude, ascension. Oof, that's a mighty steep mountain on this card. But swords are all about our thoughts, so it may be your perspective that's making that mountain appear so daunting.

ROPE: confinement, control, will, joining, ascension. It's important to keep in mind that ropes not only bind and confine, but they can also be a tool to pull yourself up and out of a negative situation. It's possible you are not as limited as you may feel.

SWORDS: element of air, intellect, power, discernment, decisiveness, truth, impartiality, purification, finality. This wall of swords stuck in the ground is grouped with an opening among them. This suggests that even though you may feel trapped, there is a way out. As the Swords suit deals with the mental realm, it may be your own negative thought patterns keeping you "trapped." Shifting your thoughts to more positive ones may provide the opening you need. If you're not feeling very positive right now, your best strategy might just be to "fake it till you make it."

WATER: emotions, life, movement, ebb and flow, power, depth, intuition, subconscious. The water here can be seen as stagnant, reflecting the stuck energy of this situation. But water is an immensely powerful force with an ability to sculpt the land itself, carving valleys and gorges out of sheer rock. In that sense, the water symbolizes the need to take back your power in this situation.

QUICK TAKES: Feeling trapped in your circumstances, feeling smothered in a relationship, having a victim mindset, refusing to see options around you. Limiting beliefs are keeping you stuck. Indicates a choice to stay stuck, giving away your personal power. Be open to alternative solutions.

REVERSED: *taking back control of your life, freeing yourself from a self-imposed prison, ability to see the way out of a bad situation.*

9 of Swords

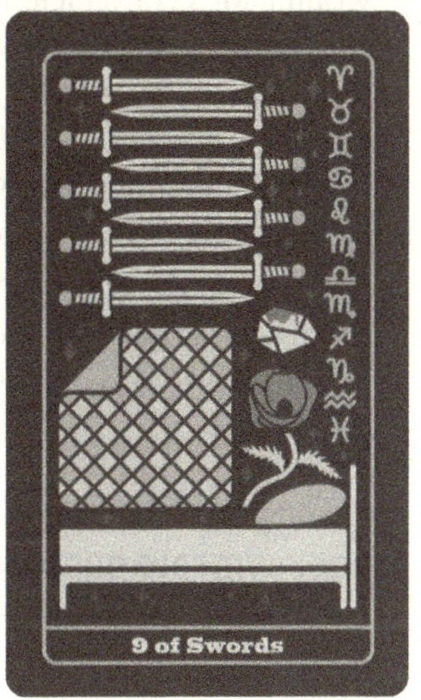

KEYWORDS: nightmares, anxiety, anguish, worries, despair, recovery, solace, hope, overcoming

ASSOCIATIONS

Astrological: Gemini

Planetary: Mars

Elemental: air

Symbols

ASTROLOGICAL SIGNS: All 12 signs of the zodiac are included on this card, which indirectly means every single human being is represented here. When we are in the midst of despair, its easy to feel isolated and alone. But the 12 zodiac signs remind us of the bigger picture. We are part of something larger and are connected to others on this planet as well as the cosmos.

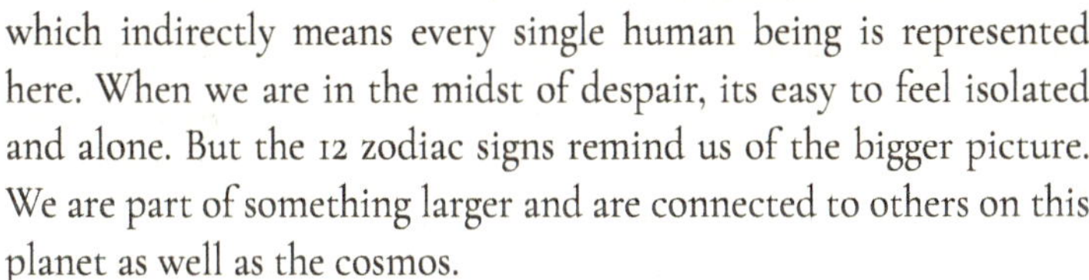

BED: sleep, rest, comfort, dreams. Here, the typical associations of a bed are flipped on their head. Instead of restful sleep and peaceful dreams, this card indicates nightmares and sleep interrupted by anxious and desperate thoughts.

POPPY: peace, sleep, remembrance, death. Poppies are the signature flower of the Greek god of sleep Hypnos. And rightly so: the poppy plant produces opium, a powerful sedative known for its ability to induce deep sleep. But too much opium can also bring about death, which is likely why poppies were also said to grow in the Underworld. Hypnos had several sons, all of whom were responsible for different types of dreams. His son Phobetor specifically caused nightmares, the kind which are very likely depicted in the 9 of Swords. The deep anguish indicated by this card may have you wishing for a convenient opium den just down the block where you could dull the emotional pain you are feeling. But as the poet Robert Frost once wrote, "the best way out is always through."

QUILT: comfort, joining, layers. I see this quilt as a patchwork of dark thoughts. When we are in a positive mental state, a disturbing or upsetting thought might flit through our brain, but we can easily dismiss it. When we are deep in a bout of anxiety or depression, the dark thoughts accumulate, knitting together to form a larger, overwhelming narrative in our mind. Much like the quilt, it covers our entire mental sphere for a time, blocking out the light.

ROCK WITH BLOODSTAIN: In the RWS tarot, the bed is decorated with a carving of what appears to be a murder scene. This may be indicative of the intensely dark thoughts that currently plague your mind. But what exactly is happening in this murderous vignette? One theory is that this scene depicts the very first murder as told in the Bible—Cain slaying his brother Abel. The ruling sign of this card is Gemini, the twins. While Cain and Abel were not twins, they were siblings—a duality. And on a deeper level, it could be that Cain represents Abel's shadow self. We all have a shadow side and living in fear of it certainly disturbs our peace.

SWORDS: element of air, intellect, power, discernment, decisiveness, truth, impartiality, purification, finality.

QUICK TAKES: Worries that keep you up at night, being plagued by nightmares, insomnia, PTSD (post-traumatic stress disorder), a need to share your burdens with a counselor or trusted friend, deep remorse or guilt weighing on your mind, time for a mental health check-in, making a mountain out of a molehill, self-harm, chronic pain.

REVERSED: *worries and stress lessening, healing from trauma, the worst is over.*

10 of Swords

KEYWORDS: betrayal, pain, endings, drama, victim mindset, resistance, regeneration, perseverance

ASSOCIATIONS

Astrological: Gemini

Planetary: sun

Elemental: air

Symbols

BLOOD: life, vitality, regeneration, essence, oath, suffering, sacrifice, gift. The wavy red line near the bottom of the card represents the blood that has been spilled from the wounds caused by the 10 swords. In the tarot 10s represent the completion of something or the end of a cycle. The blood indicates that there has been suffering and struggle as you near this completion. But as Swords are the suit of the mental realm, the suffering has more likely come from your thoughts than from your body. A wide variety of ancient cultures enacted blood sacrifices to honor and appease their gods and goddesses. Jesus Christ's crucifixion can be seen as the ultimate blood sacrifice for the good of humanity. The blood here can be seen to pose the question, "What can you give up or sacrifice for the betterment of your situation?" Blood can also be donated and willfully given as a gift—this symbol can indicate the potential gifts that may come to you through the new beginning ushered in by the 10 of Swords.

Blood has an amazing ability to regenerate. If you donate blood or lose blood from a wound, it only takes two days for the plasma to be replaced, and only a matter of weeks before your complete blood volume has been regenerated. In this way, the blood symbolizes that no matter how much loss you've experienced through your struggles, there is hope for regeneration and growth.

One last fun fact: there are approximately 10 pints of blood in the average adult body. So that's 10 pints, 10 swords . . . you can't make up this kind of synchronicity!

HAND GESTURE: blessing, mystery. In the RWS tarot, this hand gesture is being made by a figure lying face down on the ground with 10 swords stuck in their back. The scene is grim—it appears the individual has died from their many wounds. But this hand gesture suggests that there's life in those old bones yet. ("Dead men tell no tales," and they also rarely make intricate hand gestures.) So first and foremost, the presence of this gesture indicates that all is not lost and that the struggles that have occurred up to this point have not fully leveled you. This gesture is also identical to the one that appears on the Hierophant card, suggesting that there are blessings to come from this cycle of completion, as well as spiritual elevation. This gesture is also considered to mean "all you see is not all that there is." This is not a gruesome death scene but rather a hopeful dawn of a new day.

The configuration of the fingers is also very similar to a mudra called *kapithaka* used in Indian dance. One of the meanings I discovered for this mudra is "return." Things may never be exactly the same after this profound event, but you will experience a return to self as you assimilate the lessons you've learned and emerge stronger.

MOUNTAINS: aspiration, courage, challenges, obstacles, retreat, perspective, solitude, ascension.

SUN: life force, joy, optimism, vitality, health, growth, cycles, illumination, masculine principle. Take heart, this sun symbol is in the process of rising, representing the dawn of a new day. There's a lovely quote by Sumit Sharma that's fitting here: "A night can never defeat the sunrise." In similar fashion, the darkest moments of our lives can never truly defeat our own inner light.

SWORDS: element of air, intellect, power, discernment, decisiveness, truth, impartiality, purification, finality.

WATER: emotions, life, abundance, movement, ebb and flow, purification, power, depth, intuition, subconscious.

QUICK TAKES: A painful ending, hitting rock bottom, a betrayal you didn't see coming, the final blow from a painful situation, playing the victim, a "woe is me" mentality, back pain and back problems. Things aren't as bad as they seem, the dawn of a new day after a difficult time.

REVERSED: *refusing to move on when it's clear you need to, moving on from a painful event, learning to trust again after a betrayal, learning new coping mechanisms, pain and sadness coming to an end.*

Page of Swords

KEYWORDS: ideas, truth, communication, enthusiasm, curiosity, learning, good news, unproductive, miscommunication, lies, bad news

ASSOCIATIONS

Astrological: none

Planetary: none

Elemental: air, earth

Symbols

ARROW: In the RWS tarot, the Page faces left while their body and feet face right. Looking to the left indicates looking to the past, while right is the direction of the future. The agile-brained Page of Swords simultaneously learns from the past while idealistically planning for the future.

BIRDS: element of air, freedom, unrestricted, possibility, enlightenment, lightness, messenger. All the Pages act as messengers heralding news coming your way. This association is reinforced here by the symbolic inclusion of birds. Birds such as pigeons and doves have been used since ancient times to deliver messages over long distances.

BOOTS: action, journey, travel, grounding, connection to the earth, consciousness, civility, protection. The red color of the boots symbolizes the passionate spirit of the Page. Red is also the color of the root chakra—the boots represent that this Page may have their head in the clouds but their feet are firmly planted on the ground.

CLOUDS: element of air, thoughts, constancy of change, turbulence, elevation, dreams. The variety of clouds shown on this card represent the quickly shifting thoughts of the Page. Filled with enthusiasm for learning new things that will excite their mind, they may bounce from study to study for a time to come. Their continuous search for knowledge will instill in them the ability to weather life's storms with agility.

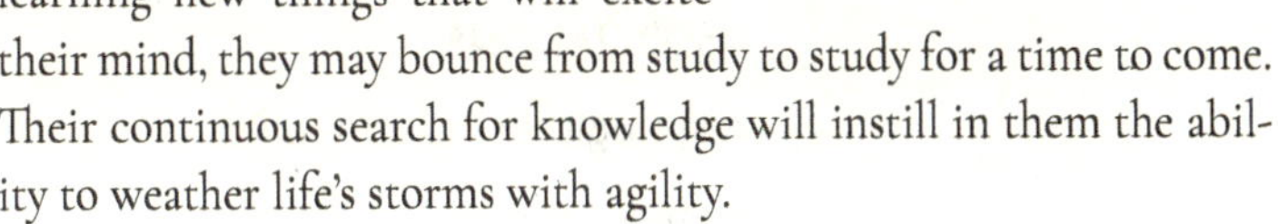

GREEN LANDSCAPE: fertility, abundance, growth.

SWORD: element of air, intellect, power, discernment, decisiveness, truth, impartiality, purification, finality.

TREE: growth, lushness, potential, sustainability, expansion, ascension. Swords are the suit of the mental realm as well as the suit associated with the element of air. The windblown tree here indicates that the Page's thoughts are full of energy and fresh ideas rush through their brain in a constant state of flux.

TUNIC: The red tunic of the Page represents the passion and vitality they bring to their ventures. As Swords are the suit of the mental realm, this Page also brings that passion to their zest for learning.

QUICK TAKES: New ideas and new projects. Be open-minded, learn a new way of doing something, speak up for yourself or for another. Indicates different learning styles, learning a new language, developing new ways of communicating, legal careers or law school, swearing an oath, a clever child that keeps you on your toes. Good news is coming your way.

REVERSED: *not speaking your truth, telling big fish stories, being careless with your words, gossip, a bit of bad news.*

Knight of Swords

KEYWORDS: courage, tenacity, drive, focus, action, push, laziness, inaction, restless mind, lack of focus

ASSOCIATIONS

Astrological: Taurus, Gemini

Planetary: none

Elemental: air, fire

Symbols

ARMOR: protection, shield, strength, self-preservation, preparation, truth, chivalry, honor, mirroring. All of the expected noble, chivalrous stuff applies to the armor symbolism in the Knights of the tarot. But another layer of meaning that can be attributed to the armor in the Knight of Swords: armor has a highly reflective surface that, on a spiritual level, can act as a mirror of sorts. The Knight of Swords has an enviable sense of drive that we may not always feel we possess ourselves. The next time this Knight pops up in a reading, consider the armor representative of a mirror: gaze at yourself as having just as much drive, strength, and bravery within you as this battle-ready Knight.

BIRD: element of air, freedom, unrestricted, possibility.

BUTTERFLIES: element of air, transformation, evolution, beauty, thought, fleeting, stages, change, self-reflection, rising above, soul. Just as the butterfly undergoes dramatic change in a short amount of time, likewise this Knight signals that big change can occur rapidly, but only when propelled by sheer force of will.

CLOUDS: element of air, thoughts, turbulence, elevation, dreams. Clouds represent the element of air, the ruling element of the suit of Swords. All four of the Knights are also tied to the element of fire. What happens when wind blows on a brush fire? It adds oxygen and can push the flames farther than they would go without it. This describes the energy of the Knight of Swords. The combination of air and fire can add to the drive and push associated with this card, but it can also enable the fire to rage out of control. A delicate balance is needed to harness this power. That is why there are both gray storm clouds and white clouds depicted on this card.

FEATHER: element of air, freedom, travel, ease of movement, change of direction, thought, spiritual evolution. In addition to reinforcing the element of air and the mental realm associated with the suit of Swords, the feather also represents the swiftness of this Knight as he rushes forward in his pursuits. The red color of the feather is also symbolic of fire, the element associated with all the Knights.

HEARTS: love, romance, sexuality. I included the hearts here to symbolize the potential for romance this Knight signifies when he pops up in a reading. With the swift energy of this Knight, you might just be swept off your feet.

HORSE: hard work, achievement, status, momentum, movement, freedom, power, solar energy. Though this white horse bears no wings, I can't help but associate it with the Greek winged horse, Pegasus. The Knight of Swords is associated with both air and fire. Pegasus is naturally linked to the air, what with that fabulous ability to fly and all. But he is also associated with fire, due to the role he played in delivering lightning bolts to Zeus. He was also known to be quite wild and difficult to tame—a quality reflected in this Knight as well.

SWORD: element of air, intellect, power, discernment, decisiveness, truth, impartiality, purification, finality.

TREE: growth, lushness, potential, sustainability, expansion, ascension. The windblown tree found here suggests the fast-paced, swift energy brought forth by this Knight.

QUICK TAKES: Change is in the air; a storm may be coming but you've got this. Heed the call to action, keep your eye on the prize, face your fears head-on, rush in headfirst. Being driven to succeed means pushing forward amid obstacles.

REVERSED: *lack of direction and purpose, a need to rest and recharge to avoid burnout, ADHD or other conditions making it hard to focus, pushing forward too aggressively, bullying.*

Queen of Swords

KEYWORDS: wisdom, logic, straightforwardness, independence, communication, sharp wit, critical, overly emotional, coldhearted

ASSOCIATIONS

Astrological: Virgo, Libra

Planetary: none

Elemental: air, water

Symbols

ANGEL: blessings, love, divinity, protection, messages. The winged being on this card may very well be an angel. Blessings certainly accompany wisdom and intelligence, which the Queen possesses. But it may also be a sylph. A sylph is a spirit of the air, first made famous in *Liber de Nymphis* written by Paracelsus, a renowned 16th-century Swiss-German occultist. Sylphs are invisible but known to have power over the air, particularly the wind and clouds. They are also known to possess a type of intelligence lacking in mere mortals, making them an apt symbol for the supremely intelligent Queen of Swords. As the tarot is rich in alchemy-based symbolism, it's worth noting that sylphs were a frequent character found in alchemical manuscripts (as were the other elementals: salamanders for fire, undines/mermaids for water, and gnomes for earth).

BIRD: element of air, freedom, unrestricted, possibility, enlightenment, messenger. For the straightforward Queen of Swords, a bird is an apt symbol to represent the freedom and lack of restriction she has with her words. The Queen of Swords has an uncanny ability to tell it like it is without being constrained by emotions or doubt.

BRACELET: While this is not a widely touted theory, there is some concurrence that this bracelet is a Victorian mourning bracelet. During the Victorian era, jewelry of all kinds intended to commemorate a lost loved one (especially a spouse) were a popular accessory. The styles varied greatly but could include special trinkets or small pictures of the loved one. Some jewelry was even created from intricately woven bits of their hair. This is an intriguing possibility as the Queen of Swords is also believed in some circles to be a widow. Just as all things in the tarot, this association doesn't have to allude to an actual death. It can symbolize someone who has gained wisdom from the hardships they've experienced in their life. It can also symbolize an aloneness that is less about being lonely and more about a fierce sense of independence. In the RWS tarot, the Queen is also turned facing the right, indicating looking toward the future. Perhaps the bracelet then represents a fiercely determined focus on the future that allows a metaphorical "death" of the past.

BUTTERFLIES: element of air, transformation, evolution, beauty, thought, fleeting, stages, change, self-reflection, rising above, divine feminine, soul. The butterfly's quick movement and fleeting nature is a fitting representation of the mental realm which the Queen of Swords rules over—thoughts flit in and out of our mind and constantly evolve and change as we learn and grow. The direct, tell-it-like-it-is nature of the Queen of Swords can be intimidating to those who don't know her. But the butterflies remind us that there is a soft side to this Queen and that there is beauty in learning to speak our truth. On another note, if this card pops up in a love reading, the butterfly's association with love and marriage may just point to wedded bliss, provided there is an understanding and mutual respect for any need for independence within the relationship. It's also worth noting that the butterfly mimics the shape of the thyroid, which resides at base of the throat. In the chakra system, this whole area is governed by the throat chakra, the energetic center that governs our ability to use our voice. Without a doubt, this blunt Queen speaks her truth with ease.

CLOUDS: element of air, thoughts, silver linings, elevation, dreams, divinity. Clouds are an apt symbol of how our thoughts float through our shifting minds and change constantly. And just as two people can gaze upon the same cloud and see two completely different things, they may also see different things in the same situation. With the authoritative command the Queen of Swords has over the mental realm, she can inspire us to hone our thoughts and help us choose to see the best in the world.

CROWN: elevation, mastery, power, royalty, sovereignty, authority, intellect, divinity. The crown of the Queen of Swords is adorned with butterflies, reinforcing that she rules with a soft touch.

MOON: intuition, cycles, emotions, divine feminine, the subconscious, shadow work, reflection.

SWORD: element of air, intellect, power, discernment, decisiveness, truth, impartiality, purification, finality. As a personality, the Queen of Swords could be described as someone who does not mince words. You won't find any false flattery here. While her brand of directness may feel abrasive to some, she concerns herself more with the truth. The sword she wields can be seen as a powerful tool to cut through the BS in any situation and get straight to the facts.

WATER: emotions, life, abundance, purification, power, depth, intuition, subconscious. Waterfalls tend to be indicative of more power and force than that of a calm stream or river. Here, the waterfall represents the Queen's ability to control the powerful forces of both her emotions and mind.

QUICK TAKES: Speak your truth. Logic prevails. Lead with the head, tell it like it is; write a pros and cons list; it's a time to make sound decisions without emotion. Indicates someone who is direct and doesn't sugarcoat things, constructive criticism, a mature and wise older woman, a widow.

REVERSED: *responding overly emotionally to a situation that needs level-headedness, a cold or overly critical maternal figure, cattiness and vindictiveness in the workplace or a friend group, anger management issues.*

King of Swords

KEYWORDS: intellectual, logic, thinker, genius, truth, communication, uncompromising, fairness, action without emotion, power, cruelty, abuse of power

ASSOCIATIONS

Astrological: Capricorn, Aquarius

Planetary: none

Elemental: air

Symbols

ANGEL: blessings, love, divinity, protection, messages. The winged being found on this card may very well be an angel. Blessings certainly accompany mastery over a realm, which this King has achieved. But it may also be a sylph. A sylph is a spirit of the air, first made famous in *Liber de Nymphis* written by Paracelsus, a renowned 16th-century Swiss-German occultist. Sylphs are invisible but known to have power over the air, particularly the wind and clouds. They are also known to possess a type of intelligence lacking in mere mortals, making them an apt symbol for the supremely intelligent King of Swords. As the tarot is rich in alchemy-based symbolism, it's worth noting that sylphs were a frequent character found in alchemical manuscripts (as were the other elementals: salamanders for fire, undines/mermaids for water, and gnomes for earth).

BIRDS: element of air, freedom, unrestricted, possibility, ascension, enlightenment, messenger, information, intellect. In the RWS tarot, the King of Swords is depicted with two very small birds in the background of the landscape. While they appear so tiny that it's hard to distinguish a specific breed, multiple sources suggest they are meant to represent Huginn and Muninn, the ravens of the Norse god Odin. In the Norse worldview, the self is comprised of multiple parts that can detach from one another under certain circumstances. More than just feathered pets, Huginn and Muninn were considered to be aspects of Odin materialized into concrete form. Known to be highly intelligent birds, the names of these special ravens translate to "thought" and "memory." (What a fitting association with the mental acumen of the King of Swords.) Odin would send the pair out every morning to travel the world and then return to him with information that could be added to his already vast store of knowledge and wisdom. Therefore, the ravens offer up a dual symbolism of communicative messengers as well as thought and intellect—all qualities the King of Swords has in spades.

BUTTERFLIES: element of air, transformation, evolution, beauty, thought, fleeting, stages, change, self-reflection, rising above, soul. At first glance, the butterfly may seem like an odd accompaniment to the serious energy of the King of Swords. But it's actually quite an apt symbol for this king. The King of Swords has mastered the realm of thought and intellect. Mastery of any realm cannot be attained without painstaking change and evolution. Just as the butterfly has attained its highest form (through some downright gooey transformations no less), so has this King. The butterfly's quick movement and fleeting nature also represents our thoughts—flitting in and out of our mind and constantly evolving and changing as we learn and grow.

CLOUDS: element of air, thoughts, elevation.

CROWN: elevation, mastery, power, royalty, sovereignty, authority, intellect, divinity.

MOON: divine feminine, the subconscious, shadow work, reflection, hidden information. On one hand, the moon represents a much-needed dash of divine feminine energy required to balance the rigidly masculine energy of the King of Swords. On the other hand, the crescent moon mimics the shape of a sickle, a tool used to harvest wheat. As the King of Swords is the master of the mental realm, the moon can be seen to symbolize his ability to reap the harvest of the mind's potential.

MOUNTAIN: aspiration, courage, challenges, obstacles, retreat, perspective, solitude, ascension.

SWORD: element of air, intellect, power, discernment, decisiveness, truth, impartiality, purification, finality.

TREE: growth, lushness, potential, sustainability, expansion, ascension, time. Keeping in line with the link to Odin (as seen with the bird symbols on this card), this tree can be interpreted to represent Yggdrasil, the World Tree of Norse legend. This also ties back to the story laid out on the Hanged One card. Just as Odin is considered to be a relentless seeker of knowledge, so too is the King of Swords. As the master of the mental realm, we can almost imagine that he would go to similar extreme lengths as Odin and hang from this tree if it meant he would be gifted with even greater knowledge.

QUICK TAKES: Mastery of the mind, a keen ability to see the truth; seek legal counsel; an expert in the field; authority figure; completion of a degree or project; a master communicator.

REVERSED: *abuse of power, absentee father figure, sociopath, dictator, lacking a moral compass.*

Pentacles

Ace of Pentacles

KEYWORDS: beginnings, prosperity, manifestation, abundance, delays, poor planning, financial stress

ASSOCIATIONS

Astrological: all earth signs—Taurus, Virgo, and Capricorn

Planetary: none

Elemental: earth

Symbols

CLOUD: element of air, silver linings, elevation, dreams, divinity. All of the Aces in the tarot offer a gift or opportunity seemingly "out of the blue." The cloud symbolizes that this gift is divine in nature, heaven sent.

GARDEN ARCH: stability, lush growth, threshold, new beginnings, expansiveness. Passing through an arch is a symbol of rebirth—leaving the old behind and entering the new. Aces in the tarot usher in positive new beginnings. As this garden arch is lush with green plant life, you can be sure this new beginning will be filled with abundance.

GRASS: elements of earth and water combined, growth, expansion.

HAND: giving, receiving. All of the Aces in the RWS tarot depict a disembodied hand emerging from the clouds. It represents a gift of a divine nature being offered when this card appears. You'll notice that a right hand is shown. Energetically, the right hand is considered to be the hand that gives energy, and the left hand receives. A gift must be accepted willingly, though, and an outstretched hand is what physically accepts a gift that is offered. So the hand also serves as a reminder that it is up to you to take advantage of the gifts and opportunities being offered to you at this time.

LILIES: purity, virtue, innocence, knowledge, fertility. The Ace of Pentacles heralds a new beginning. When something is new and fresh, it is inherently innocent and pure—the symbolic qualities of the lily. I also believe the lilies here represent fertility. Figuratively, these flowers indicate that this new beginning is bound to financially or materially bear fruit. Pentacles are the suit of the physical realm and Aces indicate a new beginning, a gift or something to be gained in their corresponding realm. So on a more literal level, the Ace of Pentacles can herald an actual pregnancy.

MOUNTAINS: aspiration, courage, ascension. While the mountains of this deck sometimes represent challenges and obstacles, in this card they simply symbolize the great heights you can reach when you set your mind to it.

PENTACLE: element of earth, physical or material realm, money and material possessions, five elements, harmony, protection, nature, feminine principle. The Greeks considered the pentagram (the five-pointed polygon found on the inside of the pentacle) a perfect symbol, representing the four classical elements (fire, water, earth, and air) plus the fifth element of spirit that brings a sense of unity to all elements. In the five-pointed pentacle, that sense of unity is even stronger. The addition of the circle surrounding the pentagram in the pentacle symbol can be seen to represent the universe, which not only contains all five elements but also unifies them. The Pythagoreans, followers of the Greek mathematician and philosopher Pythagoras, called the pentagram *hugieia*, which translates to "health." All of the Aces in tarot can be seen as a gift, and with Pentacles being the suit of the physical realm, this Ace reminds us that good health is truly a gift.

ROSE: passion, vitality, unfolding, magic, illumination, transformation. The lush, unfolding petals of the rose are symbolic of the new beginning unfolding for you right now. Additionally, when we see the combination of roses and lilies together on a card, they indicate a balancing act between the energies of the spiritual realm (lily) and the energies of the material realm (rose). Pentacles are the suit of the material realm, but this gift offered by the Ace of Pentacles comes from the spiritual realm.

QUICK TAKES: Windfall in any area of life; all systems go; a new job offer or business opportunity; abundant wealth and good fortune; the gift of good health. Your manifestation game is strong, the world is your oyster. Indicates banking and entrepreneurial professions; a seed that needs sowing; a pregnancy.

REVERSED: *a financial opportunity falls through, be careful with your finances, delays in attaining your goals.*

2 of Pentacles

KEYWORDS: balance, change, options, adaptability, juggling, flux, overextension, fluctuation

ASSOCIATIONS

Astrological: Capricorn

Planetary: Jupiter

Elemental: earth

Symbols

BOATS: navigation, inner compass, journey, transition, refuge. These poor little ships are navigating some pretty choppy waters. You'll notice, however, that they are still managing to stay afloat just fine, symbolizing that we too can be resilient in the face of rough times.

HANDS: The hands here are shown juggling two pentacles, indicating a need to find balance in some area of your life.

HAT: role, persona, thoughts, status. What an unusual red hat we find on this card. The traditional hat worn by performing jugglers looks similar in shape, so this hat may be intended to reinforce the juggling energy of this card. But they are not typically exaggeratedly tall like this one. Let's not beat around the bush: this hat has a definite phallic aspect to it. But why on this card? As this card is a two, one association with overt masculine energy may tie back to the Qabalistic Tree of Life. Chokmah is the second sephirah on the Tree of Life. It is located on the right side of the diagram, and all of the sephirot on the right side are associated with force and masculinity.

It may be that the hat implies a need to take aggressive action in order to get your life back in balance. Or it could simply be a device to help balance the more feminine energies of the pentacles and water found on this card. Or, to be more blunt about it, the hat may be saying that no matter how turbulent your life is right now, there's no need to be a dickhead.

LEMNISCATE (INFINITY SYMBOL): infinity, eternity, perpetual motion, limitlessness, balance. The 2 of Pentacles represents the ultimate balancing act. The lemniscate reminds us that change is a never-ending constant in our lives—how we balance the ups and downs is what is important. The green color of the lemniscate (in addition to this card belonging to the suit of Pentacles, the suit of the material realm) suggests your current balancing act might pertain to finances or the body.

PENTACLES: element of earth, physical or material realm, money and material possessions, five elements, harmony, protection, nature, feminine principle.

SHOE: action, journey, travel, grounding, connection to the earth, humanity, consciousness, civility, protection. The green color of the shoe reinforces a connection to the earth. It's important to remember that even when things get a bit topsy-turvy, you can still maintain a state of groundedness and stability.

STAGE: fantasy, illusion, overdramatization, perspective, keeping up appearances, story. In the 2 of Pentacles, the stage symbol may suggest that someone is putting on an act. As this card is all about a juggling act, it makes me think of someone who is stretched too thin and pulled in too many directions but is intent on making others believe they are balancing things just fine when in reality, they are about to collapse under the weight of one of those pentacles at any moment.

WATER: emotions, movement, ebb and flow, power, depth, intuition, subconscious. The turbulent waters of the 2 of Pentacles represents the natural fluctuations we experience in life.

QUICK TAKES: A balancing act; multitasking; pulled in different directions. Change is inevitable; weigh your options carefully; remain adaptable during times of transition. Indicates fluctuations in finances, investment choices, potential for travel.

REVERSED: *stretched too thin, trying to do too many things at once, a need to bring things back into alignment, balance your finances.*

3 of Pentacles

KEYWORDS: collaboration, teamwork, apprenticeship, consistent effort, competition, lack of teamwork

ASSOCIATIONS

Astrological: Capricorn

Planetary: Mars

Elemental: earth

Symbols

APRON: craftsmanship, protection, dignity of labor, purity. The apron holds a special place in Masonic symbology. It is the first gift a Freemason initiate receives and (according to *freemason.com*) is "an emblem of innocence and the badge of a Mason."

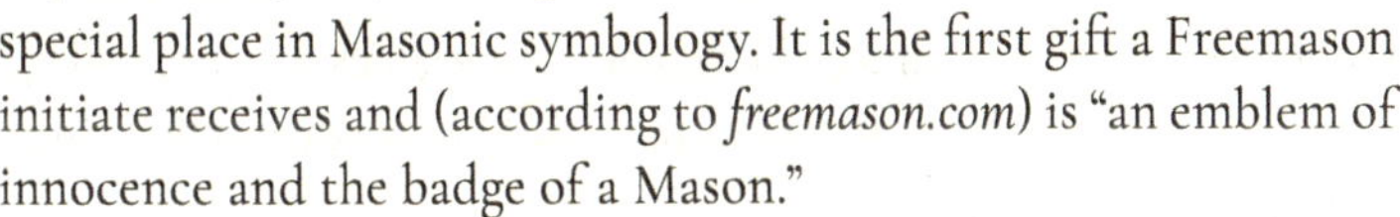

ARCH: new direction, initiation, expansiveness, balance, opportunity, mastery. The Holy Royal Arch is the third and final degree of Freemasonry that signifies the completion of the journey from "initiation to exaltation." To quote the Masonic *Book of Constitutions:* "Pure and Antient Freemasonry consists of three degrees and no more, those of the Entered Apprentice, Fellow Craft and Master Mason including the Supreme Order of the Holy Royal Arch." This evolution from apprentice to master is reflected in the energy of this card, both through the arch itself and the card's number of three.

ARCHITECTURAL PLAN: planning, building, vision for the future, manifestation. Those who actively practice manifestation know that one of the most powerful strategies for manifesting something into reality is to write it down. On a deeper level, the architectural plan symbolizes a sort of manifestation—drawing something on paper that you wish to see become a material reality. I guess you could say there's a bit of magic in architecture.

BENCH: contemplation, time-out, pause, patience, foundations. The 3 of Pentacles indicates that the ball is rolling and work is underway on a collaborative project. The bench symbolizes that this process will require patience and there will be times that you need to pause and evaluate how the project is going.

COLUMN: structure, support, balance, strength, knowledge, spiritual ascension, grandiosity.

CROSS: religion, the human body, faith, redemption, culmination.

LIRIPIPE: academic knowledge, mastery. The orange hood with a long tail is known as a liripipe. In addition to being a popular item of clothing in medieval times, it has also become associated in the modern era with academic achievement, sometimes worn at college graduations. It symbolizes the learning and knowledge to be gained from collaborating with others.

MALLET: tool, craftsmanship, labor, apprenticeship, mastery, authority. In Freemasonry traditions, the mallet is the first tool the apprentice learns, as well as an emblem of the Master, symbolizing their authority to rule their lodge. There are three degrees of Freemasonry, and the mallet represents each degree simultaneously, as well as the importance of collaboration between people with varying degrees of skill.

PENTACLES: element of earth, physical or material realm, money and material possessions, five elements, harmony, protection, nature, feminine principle. The configuration of the three pentacles mimics the Supernal Triad, the first three sephirot in the Qabalistic Tree of Life.

ROSE: passion, vitality, enlightenment, secret wisdom.

QUICK TAKES: A harmonious collaboration; combining multiple skill sets to achieve success; synergy within a team; working toward a common goal; mastery of your craft.

REVERSED: *lack of harmony within a group, not feeling appreciated for what talents you bring to the table.*

4 of Pentacles

KEYWORDS: frugality, savings, control, scarcity, greed, materialism, overspending, generosity, letting go

ASSOCIATIONS

Astrological: Capricorn

Planetary: sun

Elemental: earth

Symbols

BENCH: contemplation, time-out, pause, patience, foundations. You've probably heard the expression, "they're sitting on a mountain of cash." To "sit on" something refers to not using it or holding on to it to use at a future time. The bench here symbolizes an overly frugal strategy to finances. And while it can be wise at times to refrain from spending, it can also restrict the energetic flow of money, meaning it's unlikely more will flow to you.

CITYSCAPE: expansion, achievement, civilization, possibility, time, clutter, disconnection from nature. On one hand, a city represents human achievement as well as the passage of time. A city doesn't pop up overnight; similarly, wealth takes time to accumulate on a large scale. On the other hand, a sprawling cityscape symbolizes being disconnected from nature. Being too fixated on material things, as suggested by the 4 of Pentacles, can also disconnect us from nature. The cityscape is also depicted small, suggesting it is off in the distance. This symbolically warns of the loneliness and isolation that can result from obsessive materialism. (In other words, don't put things before people.)

CLOAK: journey, regalia, stagnation, shadow. The wearer of the cloak in the 4 of Pentacles has surely been meticulous about their choices on their journey to arrive at a place of such wealth. But the outer black color indicates they could find themselves in a place of financial stagnation if they are not careful. There is a flow to the energy of money and while being careful with your finances can be wise, there is a fine line between frugality and blocking financial flow. Black is also the color of the shadow self, so the cloak may be asking you to assess any fears or negative mindsets you may hold around money.

CROWN: elevation, mastery, power, authority, intellect, divinity. The crown holds a pentacle in it—it almost seems the wearer wants to be flashy with their wealth to appear powerful and create envy. But a kingdom based solely on riches ultimately lacks spiritual substance and is bound to fall.

PENTACLES: element of earth, physical or material realm, money and material possessions, five elements, harmony, protection, nature, feminine principle.

SHOES: action, journey, travel, grounding, connection to the earth, humanity, consciousness, civility, protection. It's interesting that shoes are typically associated with things like action and travel, because here there is a sense of stagnation and sitting still (implied by the bench). The wealth indicated by this card would probably easily finance some amazing travel, but the energy of this cards suggests instead a fear of spending the money that has been acquired. The shoes are also on top of two of the pentacles, indicating a desire to tightly control where the finances go. In many cultural traditions, walking across certain things without removing your shoes is a sign of disrespect. The shoes being on top of the pentacles suggests that even though this individual has accumulated a great deal of money, they have no respect for it. Money ultimately is energy, and respecting the natural flow of that energy is more conducive to creating abundance. Holding too tightly to money restricts the flow of energy, essentially restricting the natural flow of abundance in our lives.

TREES: growth, lushness, potential, sustainability, expansion, ascension, time. The incredible longevity of trees makes our short human lives seem like mere blips on the timeline. The oldest known living tree is a bristlecone pine that resides in Eastern California. Known as Methuselah, this nearly 5,000-year-old evergreen would have been well established when the ancient Egyptians built the pyramids at Giza. The tree symbol here reminds us that slow and steady financial growth is often the most long-lasting. And just as trees drop their leaves in the fall, to achieve true growth we shouldn't hold on too tightly to material things.

QUICK TAKES: Examine your relationship with money; fear around losing money. Money is energy; holding on too tightly to something or someone; money can't buy happiness; hoarding; placing too much importance on things; unhealthy relationship with money. Strike a healthy balance between saving and spending; slow and steady financial accumulation; savings or retirement plan; inheritance or monetary gift.

REVERSED: *overspending or accumulating debt, gambling away your money, allowing money to flow, releasing the need for control.*

5 of Pentacles

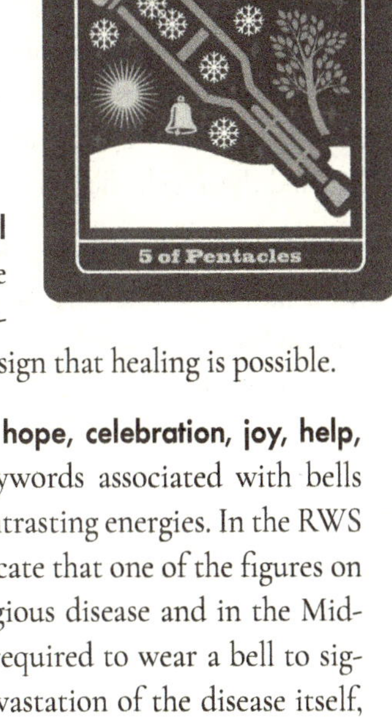

KEYWORDS: loss, despair, hardship, poverty, recovery, sanctuary, hope

ASSOCIATIONS

Astrological: Taurus

Planetary: Mercury

Elemental: earth

Symbols

BANDAGE: wound, injury, emotional pain, struggle, healing. The bandage indicates feeling beat-up by present circumstances or struggles, but it also is a sign that healing is possible.

BELL: warning, signal, stigma, death, hope, celebration, joy, help, healing. Just reading through the keywords associated with bells might perplex you—such a range of contrasting energies. In the RWS 5 of Pentacles, the bell is meant to indicate that one of the figures on the card is a leper. Leprosy is a contagious disease and in the Middle Ages, those infected with it were required to wear a bell to signal their approach. Aside from the devastation of the disease itself, the stigma around it was probably equally painful. In more modern times, it makes me think of the terrible treatment of people infected with AIDS in the 1980s and '90s—the stigma associated with the disease led to prejudices and even moral judgments against those who had it. As the 5 of Pentacles deals with themes of poverty, the bell can be seen to symbolize a similar unfair stigma associated with being poor or experiencing poverty.

Bells have also been used historically to signal death (think of the expression made famous by Ernest Hemingway, "for whom the bell tolls") as well as to herald joy and celebration at weddings or during Christmas. Both of these associations give the bell a more positive slant; even death symbolically indicates that a time of despair and hardship is coming to an end.

I also personally associate bells with sound healing and angels. I own a lovely bell whose tone is meant to balance the heart chakra and was gifted a small bell intended for ringing to call upon my guardian angels. And of course, there's the famous line from Frank Capra's film *It's a Wonderful Life*: "Every time a bell rings, an angel gets its wings." Some also say when angels are near, you hear ringing in your ears. These associations make the bell a symbol of hope, healing, and the angelic help that is always available to us if we just ask.

CRUTCH: support, humility, health issues, excuses, substitute, forward movement, healing, temporary. We all need a little support now and then, so there's no shame in using a crutch—either actually or symbolically. A crutch can propel us forward when we are limited in our movement. When we experience financial limitations, a little financial help can get us on our feet again. But a crutch can also be a limitation itself when it is used in place of a better solution. The crutch can also signify an actual health issue. If this card pops up for you while you are battling any medical conditions, know that the crutch is also a symbol of a temporary nature and can be seen as a hopeful sign that your ailments will not last long.

FOOT: action, journey, travel, grounding, connection to the earth, primal nature, lack of resources, vulnerability. The foot symbol holds similar meanings to the shoes we see throughout tarot. Our feet take us places and ground us and connect us to the earth, shod or not. But here in the 5 of Pentacles, the bare foot also implies a lack of resources and vulnerability. The blue color of the foot coupled with the snowy landscape creates an almost palpable feeling of despair—frostbite or worse may occur from this situation unless help is sought or offered.

PENTACLES: element of earth, physical or material realm, money and material possessions, five elements, harmony, protection, nature, feminine principle. The pentacles here are in the formation of the upper half of the Qabalistic Tree of Life. As the tree is incomplete, it represents the feeling that we do not have all we need at this time.

SNOW: winter, change, cycles, sadness, purity, beauty, hibernation, renewal. A little personal aside: I have lived in Colorado for about 20 years now, and I still struggle with winter. I much prefer the longer, sunshine-filled days, and wearing flip-flops (which I still occasionally do in winter as an act of rebellion). But I've slowly learned to embrace the beauty of winter as well. In winter, though things may appear dried up and dead on the surface, there is wondrous energy and growth happening underneath—seeds are germinating, and the earth is literally renewing itself from within. The 5 of Pentacles, for all of its heavy energy, can also symbolize the potential for renewal on all fronts.

STAINED-GLASS WINDOW: hope, sanctuary, grandiosity, inspiration, renewal, storytelling. The stained-glass window likely belongs to a church with shelter, warmth, and food just on the other side. Is it possible that help is closer than you think? Or maybe you are too prideful to ask for the help you need? In medieval times, stained-glass windows were made from sand and wood ash. That means someone had to be the first person to look at a pile of ashes and see potential in them. Similarly, it might be that your resources are not fully depleted, but that you need to shift your perspective on the situation. Historically, stained-glass windows in churches depicted colorful scenes from the Bible, laying out a story for the beholder. Often, a poverty or scarcity mindset stems mostly from the stories we tell ourselves. Can you craft a different scene in your mind's eye? One that tells a story of abundance instead?

STARBURST: light, hope, spiritual enlightenment. The burst of light here is best summed up by a quote by Aristotle: "It is during our darkest moments that we must focus to see the light."

TREE: growth, potential, sustainability, expansion, ascension, time. The green, lush leaves of the tree are in stark contrast to the wintry, barren landscape of this card. It is a reminder of the reliability of the changing seasons and that these hardships will shift in time as well.

QUICK TAKES: Financial hardship; economic downturn; loss of a job or home; scarcity mindset; refusing to see the solutions right in front of you; codependence in a relationship; self-sabotaging thoughts, feeling like you are on the outside looking in; leg injury.

REVERSED: *accepting the help being offered, light at the end of the tunnel, improving financial circumstances, beginning to rebuild after a loss.*

6 of Pentacles

KEYWORDS: giving, generosity, sharing, charity, stinginess, dependence, debt

ASSOCIATIONS

Astrological: Taurus

Planetary: moon

Elemental: earth

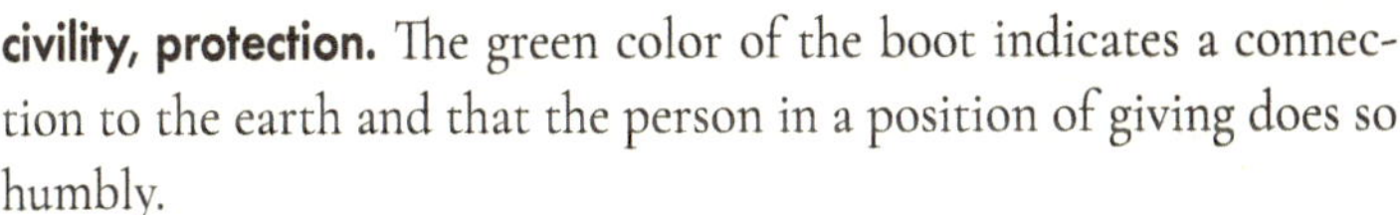

BOOT: action, grounding, connection to the earth, humanity, consciousness, civility, protection. The green color of the boot indicates a connection to the earth and that the person in a position of giving does so humbly.

CASTLE: aspirations, attainment, future reward, wealth, nobility, power, comfort, public image, refuge. The castle symbolizes the nobleness inherent in the act of giving freely when we are fortunate enough to have resources to share. There is also something poignant about the small size of the castle—who is the true owner of it? You might assume it belongs to the giver, but even the wealthiest sometimes find themselves in need of assistance.

HAND: giving, receiving. Two hands appear in this card: one giving, one receiving. This represents that it is part of the human condition to experience both sides of this coin in our life.

HAND GESTURE: blessing, wealth, abundance, root chakra. The blue hand subtly mimics the gesture of blessing seen in the Hierophant, indicating the spiritual nature of giving unconditionally. It is also making the shape of the *Kubera* mudra (named for Kuber, Hindu god of wealth), which signals wealth and abundance on all levels and is also believed to activate the root chakra, the energetic seat of our sense of security and stability.

PENTACLES: element of earth, physical or material realm, money and material possessions, five elements, harmony, protection, nature, feminine principle.

SCALES: balance, possibility, fairness. This is a card associated with charitable giving; the scales represent giving fairly and equally to those in need. But the scales can also signal a need to assess possible imbalances that might exist in your current situation—power dynamics within a relationship, distribution of wealth, and what may be expected in return are all questions the scales ask. Scales rarely stay perfectly balanced for long, so they also remind us that we all have the potential to experience both sides of the giving and receiving coin. I can't help but think of the inherent balance in the saying "you get what you give."

STAGE: keeping up appearances, story. Stage cards can indicate the possibility that someone is putting on an act. As the 6 of Pentacles is all about generous giving, the stage symbol asks, "Is this person truly giving from the goodness of their heart? Or are they merely playing the role of a generous person to garner acclaim and praise?"

TREES: growth, lushness, potential, sustainability, expansion, ascension, time. There is an expansive, rising energy inherent in the nature of giving and helping others. This spirit is captured in the symbolism of the tree as well as this lovely quote by 13-year-old community activist Elijah Lee: "When one falls we all fall, but when one rises we all rise."

QUICK TAKES: Share your wealth with others. Indicates the joy of giving, charitable donations, giving for the sake of giving, financial help offered lovingly, graciously receiving financial help, a wealthy benefactor, offering help in nonfinancial ways, expressing gratitude, a balance between give and take.

REVERSED: *abuse of power, giving with strings attached, financial scams, owing a debt.*

7 of Pentacles

KEYWORDS: patience, perseverance, steady growth, long-term rewards, harvest, fruition, lack of planning, frustration, laziness

ASSOCIATIONS

Astrological: Taurus

Planetary: Saturn

Elemental: earth

Symbols

BOOTS: action, journey, travel, grounding, connection to the earth, humanity, consciousness, civility, protection.

GRAPES: abundance, prosperity, celebration, blessings. The grapes here represent reaping the harvest of your hard work. But don't forget to also take into account the celebratory nature of grapes and make some time to rejoice in how far you've come.

HOE: hard work, effort, cultivation, planting seeds.

MOUNTAINS: aspiration, courage, challenges, obstacles, retreat, perspective, solitude, ascension. The mountains here simultaneously represent the challenges you have already overcome to get to this point, as well as the challenges ahead. For now, take a respite on this metaphorical hike and appreciate how far you've come.

PENTACLES: element of earth, physical or material realm, money and material possessions, five elements, harmony, protection, nature, feminine principle.

STAFF: support, guidance, authority, leadership, solitude. In the RWS tarot, there is technically no staff depicted. There is, however, a garden hoe. But every time I look at this card, my mind interprets the long pole of the hoe to be a staff, so I decided to include both symbols. As a solo business owner, I find this card resonates deeply with me. The individual on the card appears alone with their crop, indicating they have put a great deal of time and effort into this venture by themselves. While solo work can be very rewarding, it can also be difficult at times without the support of a team to cheer you on when things get tough. In this deck, I am including the staff to remind the solo workers out there that you are divinely supported in your ventures. Don't forget to celebrate how far you've come on this journey.

QUICK TAKES: All good things take time. Slow growth leads to deep roots; slow and steady wins the race; your hard work is about to pay off. Embrace the power of perseverance, reap the rewards, reflect on how far you've come, enjoy the fruits of your labor. Indicates long-term planning, finding yourself at a crossroads, agricultural careers.

REVERSED: *expecting immediate results, not putting in the required effort toward your goals, failing to make a sustainable plan.*

8 of Pentacles

KEYWORDS: practice, skill, discipline, craftsmanship, mastery, self-improvement, perfectionism, shoddy work

ASSOCIATIONS

Astrological: Virgo

Planetary: sun

Elemental: earth

Symbols

APRON: craftsmanship, protection, dignity of labor, purity. The apron holds a special place in Masonic symbology. It is the first gift a Freemason initiate receives and (according to *freemason.com*) is "an emblem of innocence and the badge of a Mason."

BENCH: contemplation, time-out, pause, patience, foundations. The bench here symbolizes that mastering any craft or discipline will take time and patience. There will inevitably be times that you need to slow down, pause, and assess where you are in the journey.

CHISEL: tool, craftsmanship, skill, patience, transformation. A chisel is not a tool of immediate results. A chisel carves and chips away at something slowly to transform raw material into something new. You may need to embrace the patience indicated by the chisel as you chip away at learning a new skill.

HAMMER: might, power, force, tool, masculine principle. One of the mightiest magical objects of myth is the Norse god Thor's hammer,

Mjölnir. Not only was Mjölnir used as a weapon to protect the gods and humans from the giants, but it was also a sacred object used to provide blessings. The hammer on this card indicates that when you truly put in the work, your pursuits are divinely blessed.

MOUNTAINS: aspiration, courage, challenges, obstacles, retreat, perspective, solitude, ascension. Mastering any craft, as represented in the 8 of Pentacles, requires a willingness to doggedly stay on the path, day in and day out. You may experience challenges along the way, but with perseverance you'll make it to the top.

PENTACLES: element of earth, physical or material realm, money and material possessions, five elements, harmony, protection, nature, feminine principle. You'll notice that one of the pentacles is unfinished. This represents a work in progress, as well as the idea that even a master still has things to learn.

TOWN: expansion, achievement, civilization, possibility, time. Just as a town doesn't pop up overnight, a skill takes time to master. The town is also symbolic of the saying "don't forget where you come from," when you reach big-time success through your efforts.

WOOD: element of fire, element of earth, fuel. As a symbol related to fire, the wood represents the passion and drive you bring to your pursuits. It also symbolizes the nature of staying disciplined and focused. The fire will die down at times, and it will be up to you to dig deep and find the fuel to keep going.

QUICK TAKES: Practice makes perfect; honing your craft; becoming master of your craft; finding joy in your work; creating routines that will lead to success; repetition as the key to success; pursuing enriching hobbies, a need for personally/professionally fulfilling projects.

REVERSED: *self-improvement, cultivating an inner practice, striving too hard for perfection, fixing another's shoddy work, cutting corners leads to poor quality, reassess your strategy for attaining success.*

9 of Pentacles

KEYWORDS: abundance, luxury, indulgence, accomplishment, refinement, success, financial independence, self-worth, overworked, materialism, envy

ASSOCIATIONS

Astrological: Virgo

Planetary: Venus

Elemental: earth

Symbols

CASTLE: aspirations, attainment, future reward, wealth, nobility, comfort, public image. The castle of the 9 of Pentacles symbolizes the attainment of wealth. Many of the cards that depict castles signify future potential wealth or reward. But here, you've arrived! That castle wasn't built overnight, indicating you've likely worked hard for a long time to achieve this level of success. Be sure to take time to enjoy what you've built. On the flip side, this same castle can warn against spending beyond your means. If paying the mortgage on your castle is a struggle, you're unlikely to find true comfort and joy within its massive walls.

FALCON: freedom, unrestricted, possibility, ascension, royalty, refinement, wealth, focus. These beautiful birds of prey build their nests on the highest branches of trees or even on cliff edges; they represent a spirit of ambition and "aiming high" in your goals to obtain the level of comfort and success represented by the 9 of Pentacles. Falcons have also been trained for hunting worldwide since the practice originated in Mongolia between 4000 and 6000 BCE. In medieval Europe, falconry was reserved for the likes of royalty and the privileged elite, making the falcon an apt symbol of luxury. In Japan, the falcon signifies good luck and wealth, further sealing the deal as a perfect symbol for the 9 of Pentacles.

When this card appears in the reverse position, the falcon can be seen as a warning. Just as these powerful raptors were trained in captivity by the nobility, they can indicate a need to assess whether you are a "kept" woman or man. Being lavished with luxury can be a hollow joy if you are dependent on, or controlled by, another.

FALCONRY GLOVE: protection, status, nobility.

GRAPES: abundance, prosperity, good health, celebration, blessings, sweetness of life.

MOUNTAINS: aspiration, courage, challenges, obstacles, retreat, perspective, solitude, ascension. The 9 of Pentacles suggests you've made it. You've worked hard and overcome obstacles on your path to get to the top. Enjoy the splendor of the view, you've earned it!

PENTACLES: element of earth, physical or material realm, money and material possessions, five elements, harmony, protection, nature, feminine principle.

SNAIL: slow energy, patience, self-sufficiency, home, protection, wealth, abundance. Snails are most famous for their slow speed. The suit of Pentacles as a whole has a slow energy compared to the swifter energy of Swords or the fiery, quick-paced energy of Wands. Pentacles are associated with the earth and money—plants of the earth and wealth both take time to grow. When you spot the snail on this card, let it be a message to slow down and take a moment to enjoy the finer things in life. Snails are also associated with wealth, as their shells (like cowrie shells) have been used as currency in some cultures. The ancient Aztecs believed one of the gods in their pantheon, Tlaloc, sometimes took the form of a snail. Tlaloc was the god of rain and represented the fertility of the earth and its abundance. The 9 of Pentacles also indicates abundance, both materially and spiritually.

VENUS SYMBOL: beauty, love, pleasure. In the RWS tarot, the woman's clothing has a pattern of flowers on it that on closer inspection appear to be the symbol for the planet of Venus, the ruling planet of this card. Venus is so bright and luminous that it is only outshone by the moon and the sun. This makes the Venus symbol a lovely reminder to celebrate your own radiance and allow it to beam brightly for all to see. And while you're at it, beware of anyone who tries to dim your light. In the words of Oprah Winfrey, "You can't go around dimming your light just to be walking with someone else." The 9 of Pentacles is a card that knows its worth, and you should too.

QUICK TAKES: Allow yourself to enjoy the fruits of your labor, live your best life, treat yourself, splurge on a big-ticket item. Indicates financial independence, living by your own rules, entrepreneurial success. Get outside and enjoy the abundance in nature.

REVERSED: *know your self-worth, take time out from work for enjoyment, financial dependence on another, adjust your standard of living, embrace minimalist living, part with things that don't spark joy, envying the wealth of others, a long-term mistress.*

10 of Pentacles

KEYWORDS: financial security, legacy, inheritance, family, ancestry, privilege, foundations, the good life, financial loss, family discord

ASSOCIATIONS

Astrological: Virgo

Planetary: Mercury

Elemental: earth

Symbols

ARCH: expansiveness, balance, opportunity, mastery. In the 10 of Pentacles, the arch represents the expansion of resources that has been built up over time in this legacy. It also hints at the financial mastery involved in accumulating wealth on this scale.

BEARD: wisdom, experience, maturity, passage of time. A beard takes time and patience to grow. So do family legacies and generational wealth. A dash of wisdom and maturity, as indicated by the elder's white beard, is also required to build a strong financial foundation for future generations to come.

CACTUS: hardiness, resilience, longevity, protection, defending what is yours, nourishment. Although I couldn't find a single mention of this plant anywhere while researching this card, in the background of the RWS tarot version, there is what looks to me like a cluster of prickly pear cactuses on top of the building. And what a perfect symbol to pair with the energy of this card. Cacti have some of the longest lifespans in the plant world, symbolizing the slow accumulation of wealth through multiple generations.

Prickly pear cacti are a nutritious food source, symbolizing the spiritual and material nourishment of this card. The water found in cacti is also quite bitter tasting, meaning they are not only ideal defensive plants with their prickly outsides, but they also defend what is theirs internally by making themselves an unappealing source of water to predators. This can symbolize the need to defend what is rightfully yours from gold diggers or even scheming family members (particularly relevant when this card appears reversed).

CASTLE: aspirations, attainment, future reward, wealth, nobility, power, comfort, fantasy, personal domain, protection. The castle here appears on a crest of arms, signifying that this wealth is part of a family legacy. Careful financial planning over time has likely been a key component to attaining this level of wealth with a strong foundation for future generations. On a more literal note, the castle can also suggest that inheritance of a home or property is in the cards for you.

CHILD (represented by small shoes): innocence, play, truth, generations, memories, inner child work. On this card, the child symbol reinforces the concept of multiple generations within a family.

DOG: loyalty, protection, alliance, domestication, unconditional love. The dogs found on the 10 of Pentacles symbolize that staying loyal and true to our purpose can result in material reward and fulfillment. Dogs can also be seen as a bridge between our own primal and spiritual natures, suggesting that the 10 of Pentacles is about more than mere financial wealth but also spiritual wealth and abundance.

DOUBLE-TIPPED WAND: divine inspiration, spiritual wisdom, will, conduit, harmony, perfect union, balance. Though it could easily go unnoticed due to only being partially visible in the RWS tarot, one of the individuals appears to be holding the double-tipped wand found in several of the Major Arcana cards. This adds even more symbolic weight to the 10 of Pentacles as a card of spiritual as well as financial abundance. It's suggestive of someone with high-level skills who can manifest material wealth but is also deeply rooted in the spiritual realm.

GRAPES: abundance, prosperity, good health, celebration, blessings, sweetness of life, transformation.

PENTACLES: element of earth, physical or material realm, money and material possessions, five elements, harmony, protection, nature, feminine principle.

SCALES: balance, possibility, decisions. The scales symbolize a balanced approach to financial gain. This is not a get rich quick card but rather a card of wealth that has been accumulated slowly over time and generations. It's likely that many carefully weighed decisions were made along the way to arrive at this level of financial security. It makes me think of a long-term investment portfolio that has been carefully curated to balance low- and high-risk stocks for optimum payout.

TREE OF LIFE: divine principle, personal development, universal law, inner life, energy flow, ascension. In the RWS tarot, the 10 pentacles are arranged to form a shape indicative of the Qabalistic Tree of Life diagram. I have chosen to be more direct and include the traditional Tree of Life symbol. The appearance of the Tree of Life suggests there is a great deal more going on with the energy of this card than representing mere financial wealth and legacy. I confess that even after a great deal of reading and research, I am personally no closer to fully understanding the vast depth of wisdom contained in the Tree of Life. But on a rudimentary level, I sense that the abundance that has been achieved with the 10 of Pentacles is not limited to the material realm—the inner life has been enriched as well. This brings up themes of the interconnectedness of our physical, spiritual, and mental realms. What we believe, we become . . . the essence of manifestation.

QUICK TAKES: Strong financial foundation; generational wealth; inheritances and trust funds; family home or business; family connections; domestic bliss; a relationship with a strong foundation; growing your family; adopting children or pets; honoring ancestors; acknowledging privilege; examining your personal legacy; retirement.

REVERSED: *financial loss, collapse of an empire, family feuds, breaking from tradition, gold digger.*

Page of Pentacles

KEYWORDS: ambition, manifestation, study, good news, procrastination, immaturity, laziness, bad news

ASSOCIATIONS

Astrological: none

Planetary: none

Elemental: earth

Symbols

FLOWERS: hope, new growth, happiness, beauty, unfolding, renewal. In the Victorian era, flowers were used to send secret messages and convey information. Similarly, the Pages of the tarot are considered to be messengers, heralding that good news of some sort is on its way when you draw this card.

MOUNTAINS: aspiration, courage, perspective, ascension.

PENTACLE: element of earth, physical or material realm, money and material possessions, five elements, harmony, protection, nature, feminine principle. When it comes to the pentagram, you likely doodled this exact star on your notebooks (or Trapper Keepers if you're as old as I am) as a child in school, long before you knew it had such a fancy name as "pentagram." It's an easy star to draw for children as it's comprised of just five lines and can be made in one stroke without lifting your pencil. Combined with the youthful energy of this Page, the pentacle is a sweet reminder that sometimes the shortest distance from point A to point B is a straight line (or, in this case, an uninterrupted line). Don't overcomplicate things: discover your heart's bliss and follow that path directly.

PLOUGHED FIELD: preparation, new growth, fertile land, new creative ideas.

SCARF: expression, adornment, flow, comfort, warmth. The vibrant red color of the Page's scarf indicates a passion for learning and an unlimited energy for their pursuits.

TREES: growth, lushness, potential, sustainability, expansion, ascension, time.

QUICK TAKES: Fresh financial opportunities; new business ideas; studying something new; finding joy in your studies; receiving a scholarship; turning your passion into a paycheck; the energy needed to complete your work; a message delivered from spirit through nature. Ground yourself while dreaming big, make a plan to achieve your goals, balance fun and work. Good news is coming your way.

REVERSED: *goals with no plan, losing yourself in daydreams, dropping out of school or failing a class, a bit of bad news.*

Knight of Pentacles

KEYWORDS: hard work, methodical, productivity, grounded, dependable, perfectionism, boredom, laziness

ASSOCIATIONS

ASTROLOGICAL: Leo, Virgo

Planetary: none

Elemental: earth, fire

Symbols

ARMOR: protection, shield, strength, self-preservation, preparation, truth, chivalry, honor. In the RWS tarot, the Knight of Pentacles does not appear to be actively rushing into battle unlike a few of their fellow Knights. In this case, their armor is more symbolic of methodical preparedness. It's no mistake this Knight is associated with the sign of Virgo: Virgos are notorious for having a meticulously thought-out plan and being ready for anything that comes their way.

CLOAK: protection, journey, regalia. The Knight of Pentacles dons the red cloak as a regal mantle of authority. The fiery red color indicates a readiness to go into battle, but as this Knight is one of the calmer Knights of the tarot, they do so only when truly necessary. (That red cloak will also hide bloodstains like a charm should they need to step up to a physical challenge.) Red is also the color of the root chakra, symbolically reaffirming this Knight's grounded nature and tie to the element of earth.

FIRE: energy, warmth, desire, transformation. All Knights in the tarot are related to the element of fire. This Knight encompasses all of the energy, drive, and determination represented by fire.

HORSE: hard work, achievement, status, momentum, movement, freedom, power, solar energy. Interestingly, some of the most common horse breeds that are black, such as Friesians and Percherons, have historically been used in farmland environments because of their power and muscle. This links the black horse found on this card perfectly to the earthy and hardworking Knight of Pentacles.

OAK LEAVES: wisdom, strength, endurance, fertility. While researching the mighty oak, I learned a bit of trivia that was news to me: the oak is more likely than any other tree to be struck by lightning. Interesting, yes? No wonder it is also associated with the Norse god Thor. The crackling energy of lightning is symbolic of fire, the ruling element of all of the Knights of the tarot. The ancient Druids believed the oak tree was the source of cosmic wisdom. In fact, the oak held such importance for them that they named themselves after it. It is believed the word *druid* comes from *doire*', an Irish-Gaelic word for oak tree. Interestingly, there is also a historic order of knights called the Knights of the Royal Oak. Instated after Charles II was restored to the British throne, the knighthood was intended to reward those who had been faithful to the king, symbolizing the steadfastness of the Knight of Pentacles.

PENTACLE: element of earth, physical or material realm, money and material possessions, five elements, harmony, protection, nature, feminine principle.

PLOUGHED FIELD: preparation, hard work, new growth, fertile land, new creative ideas, masculine sexuality. The earthy Knight of Pentacles brings a strong work ethic to the table, symbolized by the ploughed field. While the ploughed field of the Page denotes a more innocent connotation, the Knights of the tarot tend to be a bit more amorous. So the frisky expression "plough somebody's field" means just what you think it means.

TREE: growth, lushness, potential, sustainability, expansion, ascension, time.

QUICK TAKES: Roll up your sleeves and get the job done. Indicates slow and steady progress; the value of a strong work ethic; new job opportunities; travel for business; outdoor careers; romance with a grounded person.

REVERSED: *a need for self-discipline, not putting in the effort, being a workaholic, feeling bored with the daily grind, an undependable person.*

Queen of Pentacles

KEYWORDS: grounded, practical, generosity, prosperity, nurturing, maternal, fertility, ungrounded, disorganization, materialism, greed, jealousy, barrenness

ASSOCIATIONS

Astrological: Sagittarius, Capricorn

Planetary: none

Elemental: earth, water

Symbols

ANGEL: blessings, love, divinity, protection, messages.

APPLE: knowledge, nourishment, fruitfulness, abundance. The knowledge the Queen of Pentacles brings takes the form of deep, earthly wisdom. Like a fruitful apple harvest, she represents sustaining abundance, both financially and physically. As implied by the old adage "an apple a day keeps the doctor away," this Queen is blessed with an abundance of good health. Since all Queens in the tarot are also tied to the element of water, she is also nourished by her emotional awareness.

CROWN: elevation, mastery, power, royalty, sovereignty, authority, intellect, divinity. The unique crown of the Queen of Pentacles is topped by a winged sun. This symbol also appears on the Chariot card. The winged sun symbolizes divinity, royalty, power, ascension, and goodness. Associated with the Egyptian god Horus, when used as a hieroglyph it was said to mean "to become, to be, to create." This practical and nurturing Queen can create anything she sets her mind to—even life itself.

FLOWERS: hope, new growth, happiness, beauty, unfolding, renewal, cycles, love. This Queen is associated with fertility. The flowers symbolize her keen ability to make anything grow (including within her womb). This Queen also reminds us that, much like a flower, we are more able to create abundance when we open ourselves up to the beauty and light around us.

GRASS: elements of earth and water combined, growth, expansion, community, interconnectedness. All Queens of the tarot are associated with the element of water. The primary element of the Queen of Pentacles is that of her suit—earth. Grass is a symbol that ties equally to the elements of earth and water. (If you've ever seen a parched field or lawn, you know that grass cannot grow without plenty of moisture.) It also reinforces the lush abundance so easily created and nurtured by the Queen of Pentacles.

PEAR: the female form, abundance, fruitfulness, spiritual enlightenment, vitality. Fun fact—the pear is actually a member of the rose family. So in addition to all of its juicy goodness, it also brings meanings of vitality and spiritual enlightenment, indicating that this Queen is not only grounded in the earthly plane, she is also connected to the spiritual realm.

In medieval Europe, it was customary to plant a fruit tree to commemorate a wedding to ensure a long-lasting and fruitful marriage. Many would also plant a fruit tree for each child that followed: an apple tree for a boy and a pear tree for a girl. With this Queen's tie to the abundance of the physical realm, the pear here can hint that a possible new baby is on the way.

PENTACLE: element of earth, physical or material realm, money and material possessions, five elements, harmony, protection, nature, feminine principle.

RABBIT: fertility, gentleness, springtime, the moon. Rabbits are undeniably associated with fertility due to their prolific procreation. So, too, is the Queen of Pentacles associated with literal pregnancy as well as the fertile abundance of the earth. The Celtic goddess Eostre is also linked to rabbits. Eostre is a fertility goddess who is associated with springtime, leading many to believe that the name for Easter is derived from her. The Queen of Pentacles encompasses all of the beautiful lushness and renewal ushered in by the season.

RAM: leadership, strength, power, spring, fertility, astrological sign of Aries. In ancient Egypt, Khnum was the ram-headed god of fertility and creation, both attributes associated with the Queen of Pentacles. Khnum was also considered to be a water god, overseeing the Nile; all Queens of the tarot are associated with the element of water. Many other world cultures associate the ram with fertility: the Native American Hopi tribe, the ancient Celts, the Kalmuks (a Mongolian people), and ancient Persians, just to name a few. As the mascot of Aries, the astrological sign for people born between March 21 and April 19, the ram is also naturally a symbol of spring, an energy encapsulated by all of the lush growth of the Queen of Pentacles.

WATER: emotions, life, abundance, movement, ebb and flow, purification, power, depth, intuition, subconscious. The lush green growth of the earthly Queen of Pentacles wouldn't be possible without the help of a little water. Even as practical and grounded as this Queen is, she is still in touch with her emotions and intuitive side.

QUICK TAKES: Embrace a down-to-earth mentality. Indicates a happy homemaker; being a caretaker or mother; a loving maternal figure. Business savvy leads to successful business ventures, financial success and abundance, financial security and stability, a stable relationship. Enjoy creature comforts, get outside and connect with nature, play in dirt, discover stress relief through gardening, learn methods of grounding your energy, find careers working with animals.

REVERSED: *gold digger, jealousy and insecurity in a relationship, keeping up with the Joneses, poor money management, hoarding material possessions or money, neat freak, a cold or neglectful maternal figure.*

King of Pentacles

KEYWORDS: prosperity, security, ambition, paternal, hardworking, grounded, critical, harsh, stinginess, materialism

ASSOCIATIONS

Astrological: Aries, Taurus

Planetary: none

Elemental: earth, air

Symbols

ARMOR: protection, shield, strength, self-preservation, preparation, truth, chivalry, honor. I find it really interesting that in the RWS tarot the King of Pentacles is the only king of the four shown wearing armor. It can be argued that on a material level, the King of Pentacles has the most to lose. In addition to the financial wealth he has accumulated, his connection to the earth suggests he also has land he needs to protect. There may not be an imminent threat to his domain, but he is prepared to stand his ground in case one arises. One of the greatest skills of the King of Pentacles is self-preservation. He understands the energetic flow of money, that part of protecting his assets has him making wise spending choices. In financial matters, having some money in savings can be considered financial "armor" against economic downturns.

BULL: conviction, determination, virility, fertility, sexuality, strength, peacefulness, earthy pleasures. On the most basic level, the bull represents the king's embodiment of the astrological sign of Taurus. Those born under the sign of Taurus are typically best summed up by the motto "work hard, play hard." They are driven, stable, and hard-working by nature, but as an earth sign that's also ruled by Venus, Taureans are known to enjoy earthly pleasures and all things luxurious and cozy. Bulls are also linked to the Greek god Dionysus, who is known to sometimes take the form of a bull. As the bull on this card is also paired with the symbol of grapes, the association to Dionysus is quite strong. The King of Pentacles, like Dionysus, enjoys all manner of sensual and physical pleasures that life has to offer.

The expression "seeing red," meaning to become quickly enraged, stems from the practice of waving a *muleta* (red cape) in bullfighting in order to make the bull angry and get it to charge. I'll spare you my personal thoughts on this inhumane practice, but did you know that this is a myth? Bulls actually lack the cone cells necessary to see the color red. The colors they can see are primarily greens and blues, the very colors of the earth itself, creating another symbolic link between the bull and the king's element of earth. The idea that bulls are naturally aggressive animals is a myth as well. In actuality, they are quite peaceful creatures who only become aggressive when the need to defend themselves or their territory arises. The powerful King of Pentacles has a similar gentle nature but is not afraid to defend his land, assets, or family as needed.

You might notice I didn't include the word *stubbornness* in the keywords. Bulls absolutely represent a stubborn nature; when they don't want to do something, they just don't. (And it's no easy task to move a 1,500 pound creature who doesn't feel like moving.) But stubbornness has such a negative ring to it. I much prefer the word *conviction*. The King of Pentacles encourages you to embrace a sense of conviction and stand fast to your unwillingness to change your beliefs—you can even be peaceful while doing it.

CASTLE: aspirations, attainment, future reward, wealth, nobility, power, personal domain, defenses, protection. The King of Pentacles is the master of the material realm; thus, the castle is part of his domain. The saying "money is power" is beautifully illustrated by this castle. But the wise King of Pentacles understands that the power doesn't lie simply in the number of coins but rather in respecting the natural flow of money.

As the saying goes, "They just don't make 'em like they used to." It can easily be argued that modern building methods fall dramatically short of the impressive feats of construction of many old castles. Case in point, the oldest still-standing castle in the world, located in Northern Syria in the city of Aleppo, dates to approximately 3000 BCE. Think about that for a minute. That's 100 generations of human civilization that have come and gone like so much dust while this fortress has remained steadfastly standing. The King of Pentacles and his symbolic castle encourage us to build lasting structure and stability. It can also be seen as a nudge to ponder what we are creating in this lifetime that we will leave behind—our personal legacy.

CROWN: elevation, mastery, power, royalty, sovereignty, authority, intellect, divinity. The king's crown is adorned with flowers, linking him once again with the lushness of the earth element. As crowns are also naturally associated with the crown chakra, the flowers on the crown represent his blooming and open spiritual nature. He is simultaneously grounded and connected to the heavens. The flowers also indicate a gentle touch to his nature.

FLOWERS: hope, new growth, happiness, beauty, unfolding, renewal, cycles, love. The flowers of the King of Pentacles reinforce his mastery over the earthly realm and symbolize his ability to bring growth and prosperity to any situation. They represent the "sweet smell of success" we all have the potential to experience, particularly when we learn to manage our finances in the keen way this king does.

GRAPES: abundance, prosperity, good health, blessings. One juicy nugget of grape wisdom comes from Aesop's fable of "The Fox and the Grapes." A fox spies a delectable bunch of grapes hanging from a vine one day. He makes several attempts to leap for the grapes but comes up short. Instead of persevering, he scornfully proclaims, "Here I am wearing myself out to get a bunch of sour grapes that are not worth grasping for." This is where we get the expression "sour grapes." We all know people like this . . . the haters who attempt to belittle that which is beyond their reach. When you ascend to the level of mastery and success of the King of Pentacles, it's not uncommon for haters to come out of the woodwork. The grapes suggest there may be some sour grapes energy in your midst. As long as it's not coming from you, carry on, ignore the haters, and enjoy the fruits of your success.

PENTACLE: element of earth, physical or material realm, money and material possessions, five elements, harmony, protection, nature, feminine principle.

SCEPTER: power, royalty, masculinity, authority. The King's scepter indicates his mastery over the material realm. The orb adorning the top of the scepter mimics the shape of the Earth itself, representing this King's deep connection to the element of earth.

QUICK TAKES: The Midas touch; money management skills on point; a loving father figure; a family provider; successful business ventures (particularly in ecofriendly business models); high-level banking or finance careers; the final stage of a successful project; conservation activism; taking a methodical approach to situation; a need for discipline and structure.

REVERSED: *an overly critical employer or father figure, using money to manipulate, putting money above all else, extreme overspending.*

Index of Symbols

To Our Readers

Weiser Books, an imprint of Red Wheel/Weiser, publishes books across the entire spectrum of occult, esoteric, speculative, and New Age subjects. Our mission is to publish quality books that will make a difference in people's lives without advocating any one particular path or field of study. We value the integrity, originality, and depth of knowledge of our authors.

Our readers are our most important resource, and we appreciate your input, suggestions, and ideas about what you would like to see published.

Visit our website at *www.redwheelweiser.com*, where you can learn about our upcoming books and free downloads, and also find links to sign up for our newsletter and exclusive offers.

You can also contact us at *info@rwwbooks.com* or at

Red Wheel/Weiser, LLC
65 Parker Street, Suite 7
Newburyport, MA 01950